## The Essence of Management Series

*Published titles*

The Essence of Total Quality Management
The Essence of Strategic Management
The Essence of International Money
The Essence of Management Accounting
The Essence of Financial Accounting
The Essence of Marketing Research
The Essence of Information Systems
The Essence of Personal Microcomputing
The Essence of Successful Staff Selection
The Essence of Effective Communication
The Essence of Statistics for Business
The Essence of Business Taxation
The Essence of the Economy
The Essence of Mathematics for Business
The Essence of Organizational Behaviour
The Essence of Small Business
The Essence of Business Economics
The Essence of Operations Management
The Essence of Services Marketing
The Essence of International Business
The Essence of Marketing

*Forthcoming titles*

The Essence of Public Relations
The Essence of Financial Management
The Essence of Business Law
The Essence of International Marketing
The Essence of Women in Management
The Essence of Mergers and Acquisitions
The Essence of Industrial Relations and Personnel Management
The Essence of Influencing Skills
The Essence of Services Management
The Essence of Industrial Marketing
The Essence of Venture Capital and New Ventures

# The Essence of Managing People

Hank Williams

**Prentice Hall**

New York  London  Toronto  Sydney  Tokyo  Singapore

First published 1994 by
Prentice Hall International (UK) Ltd
Campus 400, Maylands Avenue
Hemel Hempstead
Hertfordshire, HP2 7EZ
A division of
Simon & Schuster International Group

Typeset in 10/12 pt Palatino
by Keyset Composition, Colchester

Printed and bound in Great Britain by
BPC  Wheatons Ltd, Exeter

Library of Congress Cataloging-in-Publication Data

Williams, Hank.
   The essence of managing people / Hank Williams.
      p.     cm. — (Essence of management series)
   Includes bibliographical references and index.
   ISBN 0–13–117326–X (pbk)
   1. Personnel management.  I. Title.  II. Series.
HF5549.W4956 1994
658.3 — dc20                                 93–38446
                                            CIP

British Library Cataloguing in Publication Data

A catalogue record for this book is available from
the British Library

ISBN 0-13-117326-X (pbk)

1 2 3 4 5  98 97 96 95 94

# Contents

# Introduction

## The aim

*The Essence of Managing People* is a handbook for managers which helps you to think about and improve the way you manage your people.

The management of people is a large subject. This book focuses on two key aspects and explores them in detail. They are the following:

- **Appraising performance:** Monitoring and assessing people's performance throughout the year; conducting effective formal appraisals at the end of the year.

- **Developing performance:** Planning strategies for the development of team and individual performances; effectively coaching people to help them improve and develop their performance.

The book is based on the principle that we make choices all the time about how we manage people. Some of these choices are conscious decisions. Many are not: they are instinctive responses to people and situations which are influenced by our needs, values, preferences and habits. The work you will be doing as you read the book is as follows:

- Reflect on and evaluate the choices you make.

- Explore alternatives.
- Identify practical steps you can take at work that will make you a better people manager.

---
# The reader
---

*The Essence of Managing People* will be most relevant and useful to you if you are currently managing one or more people. The exercises and activities are based on the assumption that this is the case. It is appropriate for people whatever their experience in people management: you will find it helpful whether you have been managing people for six months or for twenty years.

The book will also be useful to you if you are preparing to become a supervisor or manager for the first time. It will help you to think through the kind of manager you want to be and to reflect on your likely strengths and weaknesses. Although many of the exercises and activities will be impractical unless you know the people you will be managing, you can use them when you become a manager to help you plan your early people-management activity.

The issues addressed in the book apply to almost all situations where someone is responsible for the performance of others. This might be in a multinational corporation, a small company, a local government department or a voluntary organization. Although your work setting has an effect, many of the underlying issues of people management are the same.

---
# The reading
---

*The Essence of Managing People*, although a 'slim volume', is very dense: it covers a wide range of issues in a lot of detail. It also has a large number of exercises and activities which could take up a substantial amount of your time. So, if you are reading this book on your own and not as part of a group-learning process, you need to think carefully about how best to use it in order to meet your needs.

Here is some information that might help you to do this:

## Sequence

The book is divided into three parts:

**Part 1. Choices:** Looks at some of the background issues of people management, and the strategic choices you make about how you manage people and the factors that influence your effectiveness.

**Part 2. Planning:** Helps you to organize the way you manage people. It gives you structures for planning your appraisals and your coaching activity. The activities in Part 2 give you the opportunity to use these structures to draw up your own appraisal and coaching plans.

**Part 3. Skills:** Helps you to improve the way you interact with your people. It focuses on the behavioural skills required to manage formal and informal discussions about performance effectively. The exercises and activities in Part 3 give you the opportunity to reflect on how you manage interactions at the moment and to identify how to develop your skills further.

Each part is free standing, so if you have a particular interest in skills, for example, you could read that part of the book first. However, the three parts are interlinked, building on and referring back to each other. So unless you have a strong reason not to, it will probably be better for you to work through the book in the sequence in which it has been written.

## Activity

There are two kinds of activity in the book. These are as follows:

- **Exercises,** which ask you to reflect on your experience to date, either as a way of introducing a concept or as a way of helping you to relate the concept to real life.
- **Activities,** which ask you to plan steps or actions you will take at work to apply concepts that have just been covered or to generally improve your performance.

You must decide the extent to which you want these exercises and activities to become integral to your reading of the book. You may prefer to not do them at all, in order to get through the book more quickly, or you may prefer to devise your own ways of actively using the book.

A word of warning: it is easy to assume that because we have understood something we are able to apply it. This is rarely the case. The development of your skills and abilities as a people manager will only happen if you deliberately practise applying the things you have learnt from this book that you find valuable.

## The words

There are some words that have been used frequently in this book which need some explanation. They are:

- **Manager:** This word has been used to describe anyone who is responsible for managing the performance of others. This includes people who may not be referred to as managers in their organization, such as supervisors.

- **Team:** This has often been used to describe the group of people that you manage, even though you may not regard them as a team in the strict sense of the word.

- **Organization:** This has been used to refer to the setting in which you work, even though you might not use that word to describe it.

## My background

I am a management consultant who works with commercial organizations to help them develop the performance of their people, both as individuals and as groups and teams. This involves consultancy work to develop values and systems, and training and coaching to develop skills and capabilities. I work with multinationals and with UK companies.

I have been specializing in people management for the last six years. I have worked closely with several companies to help them develop the capability of their managers to manage people effectively. This has brought me into contact with hundreds of managers and the issues that they face. *The Essence of Managing People* is based on these experiences.

I have also managed people myself, recruiting and developing a team of training consultants for a consultancy company. Before joining the private sector, I worked extensively with local government and voluntary organizations.

# Influences

I would like to acknowledge several influences that have informed the writing of this book:

- Much of Part 3 is based on the work of Huthwaite Research Group and their behavioural approach to interactive skills. Although I have not used their systems or research explicitly, they underpin the sections of Part 3 which deal specifically with behaviour.
- The material on needs and recognition in Part 1 is based on the work of the Pellin Institute, run by Peter Fleming. In a broader sense, my involvement with Pellin has been a significant contribution to my own development as a person and as a people worker.
- The material on planning appraisals has been influenced by my involvement with John Hall in launching a new appraisal system in Sun Microsystems UK in 1988.
- The material on helping styles in Part 2 has been influenced by the work of David Megginson from the Sheffield Business School and by aspects of the situational leadership model developed by Herschey and Blanchard.

# Part 1

## Choices

Part 1 looks at some of the background issues of people management: the strategic choices you make about how you manage people and the factors that influence your effectiveness.

# 1

# What kind of manager are you?

You are a manager. This means that you probably have the following:

- Targets to achieve.
- People to manage.
- Tasks to perform.
- At least one senior manager to influence.
- An organization to liaise with.
- A distinct shortage of time!

It is a tall order. If you are to do all of those things well, in the time available, you will have to make strategic choices about how to focus your activity.

In fact, you will already have made such choices. Some you will have made consciously, as part of your planning process: you will probably have decided targets, timescales, task allocation, for example. Other choices are made less overtly: they reflect your preferences and your personality, and you make them instinctively, often without realizing how they affect the way that you operate as a manager. For example, if you are a perfectionist, this may affect your comfort at delegating work to others and the way you monitor their activity. There will be choices you are making subconsciously, as a result of the high standards you set yourself, which will determine the kind of manager you are.

# Doers and developers

In this book, we shall focus on one of the key strategic choices you make as a manager. This concerns the extent to which the way you manage is driven by the desire to develop the capabilities and potential of the people you manage.

Basically, there are two types of manager: the 'doer' and the 'developer'. 'Doers' see their job primarily in terms of *performing* tasks and achieving targets. They do not like delegating, preferring to lead by example, doing as much of the team's workload themselves as they can. For the 'doer', management of people focuses on ensuring that they do the tasks they are given in the agreed timescale. 'Doers' do not invest much time in developing the capabilities of their people. 'Developers', on the other hand, see their job primarily as *enabling* their team to perform tasks and achieve its targets. They delegate as much of their workload as they can, so that they have the time to play a strategic role within the team. Their management of people focuses on motivating and supporting them to take increasing responsibility. They invest considerable time in developing the capabilities of their people.

Although I have met managers who fall cleanly into one or other of these categories, most, in my experience, fall somewhere in between. Most managers are preoccupied with achieving their targets, just as most are concerned, to some degree, with developing their people. The labels are most useful when placed at either end of a continuum which stimulates you to think about where you would locate yourself. Use Exercise 1.1 to reflect on your own position on the continuum.

## *EXERCISE 1.1*

Spend a few minutes now reflecting on how you see yourself as a manager: are you mainly a 'doer' or 'developer'? Focus on how much you:

- Delegate work when possible.
- Invest time in developing your people.

If it is helpful, place a mark on the line below to indicate where you think you are on the continuum between the two.

Doer ............................................... Developer

Your choice about the extent to which you are a 'doer' or 'developer' will be influenced by several factors. There will be circumstances when you need to be near the left-hand end of the continuum in the exercise, and there will be circumstances when it is more appropriate to be at the other end. Some of these factors are external, concerning the nature of the work, the capabilities of the people concerned and the culture of the organization. Others will be internal, concerning your own preferences – your willingness to take risks, for example.

---

# External factors

---

The external factors bearing on many organizations in the 1990s are putting increasing pressure on managers to be 'developers'. This is expressed in different ways in phrases such as 'manager as coach', the 'facilitative manager', the 'learning organization'. There are several reasons for this trend:

- The flattening of hierarchies – there are fewer management levels, so managers have broader spans of control.
- The increase in matrix and project management structures.
- The separation of management and technical career ladders.
- The promotion of managers for their management rather than technical capabilities.
- The dependence of managers on technical experts within their teams because of the rate of technological change.

This does not mean that you should change the habits of a lifetime! It does mean, however, that the strategic choices you make about the way you manage your people should be based on a conscious and rational analysis of the requirements of your particular situation. The questions in the following paragraphs will help you to evaluate where you should be on the 'doer'–'developer' continuum.

**Will the performances of your people improve significantly if you invest time in developing them?** This depends on the potential of the people you have working for you. If the people you manage have neither the potential nor the desire to develop their perform-ance or their career, it is unlikely that being a 'developer' will be productive. On the other hand, if some or all of your people *do* have potential and motivation, investing your time and energy in helping them to fulfil their potential could benefit both you and them in the short term and the organization in the long term.

**Will the performance of the team be significantly improved if people's capabilities are developed?** This depends on the nature of the work your team does. If the work does not require a high level of capability, for example, there may be neither the scope to develop people nor much pay-off from doing so. If, on the other hand, there is scope for people to take more responsibility or to enhance the quality of their work, it is likely that there will be significant pay-off if their capabilities are developed.

**Would your performance as manager be significantly improved if you were able to delegate more?** This depends on the nature of your role as a manager. If your job is mainly to manage the activity of your team, there may be little benefit for you in delegating work in order to free up time to do other things. If, on the other hand, your job involves strategic, long-term planning and decision-making and you are constantly prevented by short-term issues from focusing on the wider aspects of this role, delegating more will be crucial to your overall effectiveness.

**Will your career in the organization be significantly improved if you develop your people's potential?** This depends on the nature of your organization and its values concerning people management. Some companies rely on the quality of their workforce and emphasize the need to develop people to ensure that the quality exists, both now and in the future. Others, rightly or wrongly, are more focused on short-term performance and less concerned with developing people's capabilities and potential. If your organization expects you to be a 'doer', it will be hard for you to buck the trend. If it expects you to be a 'developer', it will be easier for you to be one, and riskier for you not to be! Exercise 1.2 will help you to evaluate which management approach will be more appropriate for you.

Having done Exercise 1.2 you may feel that your instinctive choices about whether to be a 'doer' or 'developer' were appropriate to your external circumstances. On the other hand, you may feel that you ought to change your position on the continuum. In most cases, this is likely to involve becoming more of a 'developer'. If this is so, Parts 2 and 3 of this book will help you to achieve this change, through the way you plan your management of people and through the way you interact with them.

## EXERCISE 1.2

Spend a few minutes now reflecting on the following five questions in order to help you evaluate where you should be on the 'doer–'developer' continuum.

If you invested more time in 'developing', would there be significant benefit to be gained in terms of:

- Individual performances?
- The team's performance?
- Your performance as manager?
- The performance of the organization?
- Your career within the organization?

# Internal factors

Most managers tend naturally towards being 'doers' – particularly in the early stages of their career in management. This is not surprising: 'doing' is what they know best and it is usually through their success at 'doing' that they have earned their promotion. As you become more experienced and comfortable at being a manager, it is probable that you will gravitate naturally towards the 'developer' end of the continuum. Having said that, I have met many managers at all levels who do not invest significant time and effort in developing the people they manage. Rationally, they accept the need to do so. But there are factors which stop them from actually doing it.

These factors are often internal – to do with the kind of people we are – and we therefore tend to be unaware of the impact they have on the choices we make. Some of the aspects of our personality which will affect the extent to which we are prepared to be 'developers' are as follows:

**Trust:** Doers are typically people who only trust themselves to do a job well. They do not like to delegate work because they do not trust other people to do it to the required standard. Developers are more likely to trust people to do things well.

**Risk:** Developers tend to be more comfortable with taking risks. As a result they will give their people opportunities to develop even though there are risks attached to them failing. Doers are more likely to avoid such risks, preferring to do everything themselves.

**Control:** Doers often feel uncomfortable unless they are in close control of every aspect of their team's performance. They do not like delegating tasks or responsibility and they give their people little opportunity to take initiatives. Developers are better able to control from a distance, interfering less with their people's work.

**Satisfaction:** Doers achieve their feelings of accomplishment from doing things. They tend not to get the same satisfaction from seeing people grow and develop, which is a less tangible achievement. Developers enjoy the process of helping people learn and obtain satisfaction from enabling them to fulfil their potential.

## EXERCISE 1.3

Spend a few minutes now reflecting on the internal factors of trust, risk, control and satisfaction and the extent to which they affect your choice to be a doer or developer.

After doing Exercise 1.3 you may feel that you have strong internal forces that will undermine any attempts to become more of a 'developer'. You should neither despair nor use your innate personality as an excuse for not changing. It is not a matter of either/or, and we can all take some steps along the continuum, if it is appropriate to do so. For many of us, the first step is to recognize the barriers that are likely to stop us. If we know, for example, that our need for control is likely to prove a major stumbling block, we can build this awareness into the steps we take to move along the continuum.

## The excuses: time and skill

Rather than look at the internal factors, many managers will present two rational reasons which stop them being developers. These are:

- **Time:** There are two sides to this argument: one is that developing people is time consuming and the other is that managers do not have the time.

- **Skill:** Many managers rightly recognize that they do not have the skills to help people learn and develop. They are not teachers – they are managers.

I have a great deal of sympathy with both of these rationalizations. It is true that managers do not have much time and it is true that the 'developer' strategy is time consuming. It is often said that it will save time in the long run, but I have always found this a rather glib argument – it did not convince me when I was managing people. Similarly, it is unrealistic to expect managers to be automatically good at developing people. Coaching is a complex and difficult business which requires a high level of specific kinds of skill. Most managers have spent their working lives developing the skills of doing, and these are usually skills which will not be effective when helping people learn and develop.

But although I have sympathy, in the end these reasons must be seen for what they are: excuses. Managers will always make time for things that they feel are of benefit to them. And they will always learn skills if they feel they are necessary to the job. The question is not whether the time exists, it is whether the pay-off you will gain from developing your people will justify the investment required. The question is not whether you have the skills or not, it is whether you want to have them.

Throughout this book you will be encouraged to take small steps which will increase your activity and ability as a developer. These steps will take time. It is up to you to ensure that you only commit yourself to achievable goals and actions – working realistically within your time constraints. If you try to do too much at once, you are likely to confirm your belief that there just is not the time!

# Delegation

The choice between doer and developer is often expressed on a day-to-day basis by the decision whether to delegate a piece of work or not. Extreme doers will try to avoid delegating unless they have to. Extreme developers will delegate as much as they can. Choices activity 1.1 will help you to explore your attitude to delegation and also to identify steps you can take to move towards the developer end of the continuum.

## CHOICES ACTIVITY 1.1

Identify three tasks or responsibilities within your current workload that you could delegate. If you struggle to think of three – struggle: unless you are a high developer already, I do not believe that they do not exist. When you have identified them, make a note of your answers to the following questions (these may be different for each of the tasks/ responsibilities you have identified):

- Why haven't you delegated them already?
- How will you benefit from successfully delegating each task or responsibility?
- Who will gain from the experience of doing them (this may be different people for each task)?
- What steps do you need to take to ensure that they carry out the task or responsibility adequately?

The trouble with delegation is that it creates work! It creates work for the manager – it will nearly always be easier to do a job yourself (if you have the time). It creates work for the people you delegate to – and you may feel that they are already overloaded. So, if you are to delegate, it is important to have a clear objective and to recognize the value of delegation. There are several possible objectives, each with their place on the doer–developer continuum, as illustrated in Figure 1.1.

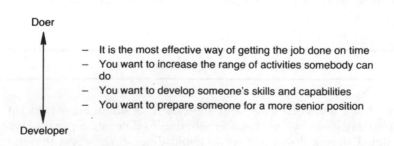

Doer

– It is the most effective way of getting the job done on time
– You want to increase the range of activities somebody can do
– You want to develop someone's skills and capabilities
– You want to prepare someone for a more senior position

Developer

**Figure 1.1** The 'doer'–'developer' continuum

Your objective will determine the way that you delegate, and in particular the amount of control you need to retain. If your objective is to get the job done, you may need to give more input to make sure that the person understands what is required and is able to meet those requirements. The further along the continuum you go, the more you are likely to give people responsibility for managing the tasks and their own learning.

The other problem with delegating is that the task will never be done as well as if you did it yourself! You will have a picture of how the task should be done – which is the way that *you* would do it. You will also have a picture of how the person you delegate the task to will do it – and the difference between these two pictures can be distressing, which is why we often decide to do things ourselves. So your objective must also shape your expectations. The price paid in lowered standards must be offset by the benefit gained from the time you have saved yourself, and from the other person's development.

When you have clarified your objective and expectations, you can plan the steps you need to take to ensure that the delegation is successful. These will involve the following two elements:

- **Instruction:** Ensuring that the other people understand: what you are asking them to do; why you are asking them to do it; how to do it (the knowledge and skills required); and what standard you are expecting.

- **Monitoring:** Ensuring that other people complete the task in the required time and to the required standard; and learn from the experience in accordance with your objectives.

The skill of effective delegating is to provide enough instruction and monitoring to ensure that your objectives are achieved. This will be explored in more detail in Chapter 6, which focuses on planning your coaching activity.

## Summary

In this chapter we have focused on a key question which will influence your reading of the rest of the book: **What kind of manager are you?** This has been explored in terms of a key strategic choice that you have made regarding the extent that you are task centred and people centred.

Most managers, doers as well as developers, are concerned to some degree with the development of their people. The key difference is that developers regard people development as a key strategy for the achievement of their work objectives. This strategy involves:

- Delegating as much work as possible.
- Creating opportunities for people to expand their skills and experience.
- Investing time in helping people to develop their capabilities to do their current and future jobs.

The rest of this book will be spent exploring these issues in more detail.

# 2

# Areas of involvement

You are a manager: you manage people. This means that, at any one time, you may have to do any of the following:

- Allocate tasks and activities.
- Check that things are being done right.
- Motivate people to work harder.
- Criticize the way someone does something.
- Understand why someone's performance has dropped off.
- Make decisions about pay and rewards.
- Give advice about career development.
- Help someone through a crisis in their personal life.

The list is endless: managing people involves a wide range of different and complex interactions, made more complex by the infinite variety of personalities, needs, attitudes and capabilities that make up your team. What a job! No wonder that managing people is the part of their work that most managers find the most difficult.

This wide variety of possible interactions, even the short list above, represents a set of choices that you will have made, consciously or unconsciously, about how you are going to manage your people. The choices are about **areas of involvement**. These areas can be summarized under four headings:

- Activity.
- Performance.

- Career.
- Life.

You may have consciously decided, for example, that you will operate as a manager on all four levels – engaging with your people on personal as well as work issues, on their futures as well as what is happening in the present. Or it may be that, instinctively, you have chosen to concentrate your involvement on managing activity. You may have decided that you will not engage in life issues, or that it is not appropriate for you to help people plan their careers. Your choices may be different for each member of your team – or they may represent a deliberate policy that you apply to everybody.

In this chapter, we will explore the demands and requirements of each of the four areas in detail in order to help you to review the choices you have made about your *role* as a people manager. Later, in Chapter 4, we will revisit these areas of involvement in order to focus on the overall objectives you set for each of the people you manage as the first step in planning your *contribution* as a people manager.

---

## Activity

---

The activity area is about what people *do* – the tasks, actions and responsibilities that make up their job. The manager's role in this area is to ensure that people:

- Have tasks to do.
- Are able to do them to the required standard.
- Have done them within the required timescale.
- Can do them again.

This is the minimum requirement of people management: all managers must engage in this area of involvement if they are to achieve their own objectives and targets. The activity area is about *quantity*: how much a person does and is able to do. As a manager, you want to ensure that people are as productive as possible. This may involve expanding the range of activities that they can do and so they may need to acquire new knowledge and skills. But your primary concern is with the *task* rather than the person. Your objective is to get the task done on time and your contribution is directed solely to this end.

The management of activity requires the ability to:

- Assess task requirements and individual capabilities.
- Match task requirements to individual capabilities.
- Explain the task requirements and, if necessary, teach the knowledge and skills required.
- Check progress, provide support and evaluate end results.

These are the basic requirements of the effective allocating and delegating of tasks and activity.

## Performance

The performance area is about *how well* people do their job. This includes tasks and activities but also other, less tangible aspects such as self-organization, communication and relationships. It is about quality rather than quantity. The manager's role is to:

- Ensure that current performance is satisfactory.
- Resolve causes of underperformance.
- Motivate people to increase their skills and capabilities.
- Create opportunities for learning and development.

In this area of involvement, the manager's priority is split: the need to get the task done well is balanced with the desire for the person to learn and develop as a result of doing it. The emphasis is more on the person than the task. Your objective is that the person improves their performance and your contribution is directed towards achieving that end. This might affect the kind of tasks you give people to do – for example, you are more likely to delegate work which gives the opportunity to develop certain skills or attributes. It will certainly influence the way you interact with them about their work, requiring the ability to:

- Clearly define the levels of performance that you expect from your people.
- Diagnose the causes of problems with people's performance.

- Enable people to learn by providing the right balance of support and challenge.
- Review people's activity with them so that they gain maximum benefit from the experience.

These are the basic skill requirements of effective coaching to improve and develop performance.

# Activity/performance overlap

The activity and performance areas clearly overlap: activity involves performance and vice versa. However, the distinction between them is important and relates back to the choice explored in the previous chapter – the extent to which you are a doer or developer. Focusing on activity tends to be a doer strategy – the emphasis is on short-term results: performances may improve through experience, but that is a bonus rather than an objective. Focusing on performance, on the other hand, is a developer strategy – the emphasis is on the longer-term objective of developing people's capabilities to increase their own and the team's effectiveness.

The different objectives dictate the kind of contribution required from you by each area of involvement. The activity area requires **management**: briefing, instructing, monitoring. The performance area requires **coaching**: diagnosing, enabling, reviewing. It usually requires a far closer involvement with the person concerned, and so more time and effort on your part. Case study 2.1 illustrates the difference between the two.

## CASE STUDY 2.1

I once observed a managing director (Brian) appraising his marketing director (Sue). The whole time was spent discussing *activity* – what Sue had done over the last year, what had gone well, what had not, and what she was going to do in the year ahead. No attempt was made to review Sue's *performance* in order to understand that the way she had done things had affected the outcomes of her activity, or to see whether she could learn from her experiences and apply this learning in the future, to make sure that the activity being planned was executed successfully.

A focus on activity rather than performance has been a feature of many of the appraisals that I have observed. It is also a feature of the way many managers choose to manage. Often unconsciously, they are concentrating their effort on activity management rather than performance development. When I gave Brian feedback, he recognized what he had done, but was surprised: it had not been what he intended to do. Use Exercise 2.1 to explore how you manage the activity/performance overlap.

## *EXERCISE 2.1*

Spend a few minutes now reflecting on the extent to which you focus on activity and performance when managing your people:

- Do you focus more on activity than performance?
- Do you spend enough time developing performance as opposed to managing activity?

# Career

The career area is about where people are going. This might involve their next move in the organization, or it might involve longer-term planning of their career development, whether that takes place within the organization or not. In either case, the manager's role is to:

- Identify the individuals' potential for career development.
- Advise them on the options that are available to them.
- Help them to choose the most appropriate option.
- Support them to achieve the desired progression.

Most managers have to involve themselves to some degree in helping people to develop their careers. This may only be an issue for you at the annual appraisal, when there are boxes or forms to be filled in! You may have to become more actively involved if one or more members of your team is pushing for promotion. Or you may positively enjoy helping people to fulfil their long-term potential.

Involvement in the career area requires the ability to help people do as follows:

- Understand their underlying needs and motivations.
- Assess their strengths and weaknesses realistically and match these to their career aspirations.
- Plan the best route for their career within the constraints of the organization and the wider job market.
- Develop strategies for achieving this plan, based on the acquisition of the necessary skills, experience and contacts.

With some of your people, your help may extend beyond planning routes and strategies. If you believe in their value sufficiently, you may decide to take a more active role in influencing their progress. This might involve creating opportunities for them to extend their experience, promoting their reputation among your seniors and peers, or sponsoring them for promotion.

Your involvement in this area will affect the way you manage activity and performance. You may, for example, delegate tasks or responsibilities as part of a career development strategy, in order to provide relevant experience or exposure. You may focus on improving certain aspects of people's performance in order to prepare them for their next positions. But your contribution is more than just management or coaching. It is **mentoring** – a combination of various ways of helping someone to fulfil potential.

# Life

Life (a rather all-embracing heading!) is being used here to refer specifically to an involvement with non-work issues which affect a person's performance or career. These might be practical and immediate, such as child-care arrangements; they might be life crises, such as health or relationship problems; they might be personal needs or ambitions, such as to have a baby, or to live abroad for a while.

The role of the manager in this area will depend on the nature of the issue, but will generally involve one or all of the following:

- Clarifying the issue and its probable impact on the performance of the individual and the team.

- Identifying realistic outcomes which accommodate the needs of the individual and the team.
- Planning how to help the individual practically to achieve the desired outcomes.
- Supporting the individual emotionally if appropriate.

Conflicting opinions exist about involvement in this area. Some managers feel strongly that people should keep their personal and professional lives separate, so that the one does not influence the other. These managers will not see it as part of their job to become involved in life issues, preferring to maintain a purely professional relationship with the people they manage. Others feel that it is impossible to separate life from work and that, if somebody has a problem that affects performance, it is the manager's problem too. At the least, the manager will want to know if there are things happening off the job that should be taken into account. At best, the manager is prepared to offer time and support if appropriate to help the person concerned to manage the issue effectively.

Organizations are increasingly recognizing that life and work are inextricably linked, that performance is affected by non-work issues and that there is pay-off in helping people to resolve these issues. One indication of this is the number of large organizations which provide the services of expert counsellors as part of the employment package. There is also a growing expectation that managers should be sympathetic and supportive when life issues arise. The increasing number of counselling courses for managers is evidence of this trend.

The choice of whether to engage in the life area is usually based on how comfortable and confident you feel about entering the personal dimension and making what is essentially a counselling contribution. Although this can sometimes be quite straightforward, with many issues it is not an easy role and can require a high level of skill just to help the person to clarify what is going on. The role requires the ability to do as follows:

- Hear and understand other people's emotional needs.
- Clarify the boundaries of the support you are offering.
- Enable others to reflect on the issues they are facing.
- Help others to draw their own conclusions about how to manage these issues best.

These are the basic requirements of the effective counselling of non-work problems.

# Overview

The four areas of involvement are summarized in Figure 2.1, which shows the objectives that can be achieved by an involvement in each area, as well as the type of contribution required from the manager. Refer to Figure 2.1 to help you with Exercise 2.2 and Choices activity 2.1, which ask you to first reflect on and then evaluate the choices you make about areas of involvement.

## EXERCISE 2.2

Spend a few minutes now reflecting on the areas in which you get involved with each of the people you manage. Write their names in the left-hand column of the table below. Then tick the boxes as appropriate (i.e. if you involve yourself with people's career development, tick the career box against their name). If it is more useful to you, grade the extent of your involvement on a 1–5 scale (5 being high).

| Name | Activity | Performance | Career | Life |
|------|----------|-------------|--------|------|
|      |          |             |        |      |
|      |          |             |        |      |
|      |          |             |        |      |
|      |          |             |        |      |
|      |          |             |        |      |
|      |          |             |        |      |

The table in Exercise 2.2 will illustrate the choices you make in terms of areas of involvement and therefore how you define your role as a people manager. It may show that you have decided to involve yourself fully with all of your people, or that you have different levels of involvement with different members of your team, or that you avoid certain areas of involvement with the whole team.

There is no right answer as to how you should define your role. Your choice will be determined by several factors which we shall

| Area of involvement | Objective | Contribution |
|---|---|---|
| Activity | • Achievement of work goals and targets<br>• Expansion of range of activity | Managing |
| Performance | • Improvement of current performance<br>• Development of new skills and capabilities | Coaching |
| Career | • Fulfilment of personal potential<br>• Motivation of individual and team | Mentoring |
| Life | • Management of disruption by non-work issues<br>• Fulfilment of life needs and aspirations | Counselling |

**Figure 2.1** Overview of areas of involvement

explore in the next chapter. The purpose of Exercise 2.2 was to help you recognize the choices you have made. Choices activity 2.1 will help you to reflect on whether these choices are appropriate.

## CHOICES ACTIVITY 2.1

Spend a few minutes now studying the table that you have completed in Exercise 2.2. Think about the people in your team and decide whether your management of them and the team would benefit if you:

• Increased the range of your involvement with each of them: for example, would she be more motivated if you spent some time reviewing her career aspirations with her?
• Reduced the range or extent of your involvement with each of them: for example, would the rest of the team benefit if you spent less time coaching him to improve his performance?

Now make a note of any changes that you think may be needed and identify a specific next step for putting each change into action. For example:

• Ask each person if they would like to meet with you to discuss their career development.
• Ask Frank if he will take over from you helping Cheryl develop her selling skills.

Most of the managers I have worked with have benefited from involving themselves more fully in developing the performances and careers of the people they manage. Most managers know this to be true. The trouble is that you are often unable to lift your head above the overwhelming mass of short-term activity management that is required. It is not even that there is not the time. It is that you do not have the time to make time! With luck Choices activity 2.1 will have helped you to lift your head long enough to identify some achievable steps you can take to redress the balance.

Some managers make the mistake of becoming overinvolved with some or all of their people. There are several versions of this, the most common of which is investing too much time on coaching people who do not have the potential to improve their performance (we will look at this in more detail in Chapter 6). The risk is that you do not invest your time so that it gives you the best pay-off. There are many managers, for example, who like getting involved in the life area, providing a sympathetic ear for their people, and who as a result spend too much time there at the expense of other aspects of their job.

If you feel, having done the activity, that you do not need to make any changes, this is likely to be because you are either an effective developer already, successfully managing your time to achieve the longer-term goals of involvement in the performance and career areas, or because your circumstances dictate that you should be a doer, as explored in the previous chapter. Either way, if you have got it right: congratulations – you are a rare breed! I would say, however, that I have met few managers who do not have room for some improvement in the way they distribute their time through the four levels of involvement!

---

# Summary

---

In this chapter we have focused on the choices you make in terms of the extent and range of your involvement with your team. These choices are the basis for how you define your role as a people manager, and involve four possible areas: activity, performance, career and life.

If you are a doer, it is likely that you will have focused primarily on activity management – making sure that the job gets done. If you are a developer, you are likely to have also focused on performance development, improving the capabilities of your people so that you can deploy them more effectively. You are likely to become more deeply involved in the career and life areas as well.

Your choices will be influenced by several factors. The next chapter looks at these factors in detail.

# 3
# Influencing Factors

So far we have focused on some of the choices you make regarding the way you manage your people. We will now look at some of the factors that influence those choices and are the context for all the decisions and actions you take as a manager. This will help you to reflect on how they affect your performance and whether you allow them to affect it too much.

The influencing factors can be grouped under three headings, and we will look at each one in turn. They are:

- The organization.
- The people.
- You.

## The organization

There are a number of ways in which the organization you work for will influence the way you work. It will have **systems** that determine how you appraise, reward and punish people. These systems will represent **policies** which shape how the organization relates to and manages its people. And these policies will be the expression of the organization's **values** and culture – a less visible factor that can profoundly affect your attitude and expectations regarding people management.

# Cultural values

It is best to start by exploring values, as they will underpin your organization's policies and systems. They will also influence the way you manage on a daily basis. Each organization has its own distinctive culture and this is often expressed in the style of management used by most of its managers. If you have worked for the same company all your life, it is likely that the choices you make as a manager will be heavily influenced by this dominant management style. If you have worked in different kinds of organization, you will probably have had to adapt the way you have operated as a manager each time you have moved to a new company, in response to the different cultural values. As a result, you will have learned a wider range of options, and will be more aware of the impact of culture on management style.

To help you think about your organization's values and the way they affect the choices you make as manager, I will give some examples in the following paragraphs of cultural values that I have come across recently in organizations that I work with as a consultant.

**The task-driven culture:** Many organisations I work with are essentially task driven: preoccupied with short-term activity to achieve targets. They are not necessarily uncaring places to work. But the emphasis is on activity management rather than performance development, which, although seen as desirable, tends to slip down the list of priorities. In task-driven cultures, the managers' effectiveness is often judged by how busy they are, so lack of time becomes a status symbol ('and how full is your diary?'). In such organizations, it is hard to move away from being a doer.

**The people-centred culture:** There are far fewer organizations that have a genuinely people-centred culture, although there are many that would like to develop one. In such organizations, managers are encouraged to see people development as a key part of their job. This is reflected in the objectives they are set and the criteria for reviewing their effectiveness. Managers are expected to help people develop their performances and careers and to organize their workloads so that they can create learning opportunities for others and directly support that learning. They are expected to be developers.

**The blame culture:** In some organizations, a lot of time and energy is spent finding somebody to blame when things go wrong. The blame culture exists to a lesser extent in most companies: an emphasis on identifying what went wrong rather than acknowledging what went right; of getting locked in to proving people to be at fault, rather than working together to find solutions. Blame cultures lead to defensiveness – and this makes performance management and development much harder.

**The 'too nice' culture:** There are organizations that have a big investment in being 'nice' to their people. This is not in itself a problem, but it can lead to a soft management style which does not do anybody any favours in the end. There are times when being ruthless is the best solution for everybody, even though it appears harsh and uncaring at the time. I know several managers who, at this moment, are avoiding taking some necessary decisions about people because they are under pressure from a 'too nice' culture (which should not be confused with a genuine people-centred culture).

**The backward-looking culture:** There are some organizations where the desire to preserve existing practices overrides the desire to improve them. This manifests itself in many different ways – my most recent example is a company that recruited people who were only capable of continuing its current activity when what was needed was people who could challenge and transform it. The backward-looking culture leads to a very limited attitude to perform-ance development: in this same company, for example, people were only trained to do what the company had been doing for the past seven years. It was felt that this was all they needed to know.

**The 'solve-it-quick' culture:** Just as there are some organizations that are into problems and blame in a big way, so there are some that are into solutions. This can be very positive, but it can also be counterproductive, for two reasons. First, the pressure to come up with a solution can lead to insufficient analysis of the problem and therefore inadequate solutions; second, the pressure on the manager to be the solution provider can lead to a directive coaching style where the manager tells people how to do things rather than helping them to think it through for themselves.

You may feel that your organzation has one or several of the above examples as part of its culture. Or you may feel that none of them describe it accurately. Use Exercise 3.1 to think about how your organization's values affect your management style.

## Company policy

Many companies have now developed some kind of mission statement. This usually includes a set of core values that says all the right things in a positive attempt to show the workforce that the

# EXERCISE 3.1

Spend a few minutes now reflecting on the cultural values that characterize your organization (these may be positive or negative):

- Identify six core values and summarize them in a word or phrase (such as 'task-driven' or 'blame'). Write these down in the left-hand column below.
- Then think about how these values affect your daily management of people. Write down against each value one way that it affects how you manage people: these could be positive or negative.

Values                              Impact

company has their interest at heart. But values do not actually *mean* anything unless they are reflected in the policies of the company and the actions of its management. The workforce will not be convinced about them until they see concrete evidence that the good intentions are being put into practice.

Whereas values tell managers what they should *think*, policies tell managers what they should *do*. An organization's policies with regard to its people can cover a wide range of issues, including grievance and disciplinary procedures, reward and remuneration, training and development strategies. For example, your organization may have a policy which tells managers that each person in the company should have nine days set aside for training each year.

Policies may be formally stated, in some form of company handbook, for example, or, at the other extreme, they can be a set of assumptions based on people's collective experience of what actually happens. To illustrate this, and the way policies can influence the choices you make, we will look at four policy issues which have an impact on your involvement in the area of performance development.

**Who is development for: the company or the individual?** Managers often ask: 'why should I invest time and effort developing someone just for them to go and get a better job somewhere else?' This is a risk: if the jobs are not there within your organization, you could lose your best people – and this could look like bad management. On the other hand; they will probably go anyway, and you will want to get the best out of them before they do.

Signalling your commitment to development could motivate all the people who work for you. But what does the organization think? A clear policy will help managers to evaluate the risks involved.

**When you say development, do you really mean training?** For many managers, in many organizations, people development involves sending people on training programmes. This will not be a stated policy, more a collective assumption, but is none the less powerful for all that. In almost every organization I work with, the personnel department is trying to change this unwritten policy so that managers use off-the-job training less and become more involved in on-the-job development, i.e. coaching. There are several reasons for this, cost being one of them. But the main reason is that learning that takes place on the job is far more effective.

**Are managers encouraged to take an active role in performance development?** If the first step is to move managers away from just sending people on training programmes, the next step is to encourage managers to become actively involved, as coaches, in developing their people's performance. This requires policy guidelines which clarify the relative priorities between focusing on activity and performance, and which emphasize people development as a key objective for managers, one for which they will be appraised and rewarded. Without these, the task-driven culture is likely to dominate the choices managers make.

**Are employees encouraged to take responsibility for their own development?** Some organizations are keen to encourage employees to take the initiative, and to move away from being passive recipients of training. In others, you only go on a training programme if you are sent, and then you regard it as an implied criticism of your performance! The current trend is to encourage people to take a more active role in their own development. Many organizations are developing learning centres on their sites, providing access to a range of self-managed learning opportunities; this is a good example of values being turned into action.

Your organization's policies on these issues, whether in the form of clear statements or vague assumptions, will influence the way you go about developing your people's performance. Exercise 3.2 will help you to clarify what the policies actually are, and the impact they have on your management of people.

## Systems

'System' is used here to refer specifically to the system the organization has for managing performance. Here are two examples

## EXERCISE 3.2

Spend a few minutes now reflecting on the policies your organization has with regard to people development by answering the following four questions on behalf of the organization:

- Who is development for: the company or the individual?
- When you say development, do you really mean training?
- Are managers encouraged to take an active role in performance development?
- Are employees encouraged to take responsibility for their own development?

When you have answered them, note down four ways in which these policies influence the way you manage your people: these could be positive or negative.

of different kinds of people management system. I worked for a small consultancy organization where, for many years, the system was simply an annual salary negotiation, based on a mutual understanding of my value to the company. In contrast, one of my clients now is a company which has an elaborate appraisal system which incorporates quarterly semi-formal reviews and the setting of targets and standards which are linked to an overall performance rating.

Both of these are management systems. Both were consciously chosen to reflect the needs of the organization, managers and employees. Both, to a large extent, worked well. But each makes different demands on the managers which affects the way they manage people. I shall now focus on five characteristics of these two different systems to provide you with a structure for reflecting on the systems within your own organization and the way that they help or hinder your people management.

**The level of formality:** The key difference between the two systems described above is the chosen level of formality. In my situation, the system was deliberately informal, an indication of the mutual trust and confidence that existed between us. The other situation was highly formalized, reflecting the needs of a much larger organization. Although formality is often necessary, it generally makes life harder for managers, because formality tends to erode trust.

**The link with pay:** Both systems were used to make decisions about a person's value to the company. Most appraisal systems are linked to pay in some way, even if only in the minds of the employees! In my situation, the discussion was blatantly about pay and was not confused with other issues. In the larger organization, decisions about pay were made as a result of discussions which were also about activity management and performance development. This can be an unhealthy combination, which discourages open self-criticism and can lead to a combative win/lose scenario.

**The emphasis on measurement:** In the less formal situation, there was little emphasis on measuring performance against set criteria in order to justify decisions about pay. In the formal situation, there was heavy emphasis on measurement, and on the collection of evidence in order to measure accurately. The need for fairness and consistency throughout the company was one of the main 'drivers' of the system. This has a considerable impact on how the manager has to manage people during the year, from setting measurable targets and activity at the beginning through to the measuring of achievement at the end.

**The value of subjectivity:** In my situation, my manager and I were great believers in subjectivity. Our mutual trust was based on confidence in each other's subjective judgments. One aim of the formal system is to reduce the role of subjectivity, because of problems with inconsistency (one manager's criteria are not the same as another's). The trouble is that no system can be totally objective: at some point it hinges on the manager's subjective judgment. Formal systems help managers by making sure they have the hard data to back up their opinions. The risk is that the emphasis on measurement and consistency suppresses the effective use of subjectivity.

**The focus on development:** One of the features of my situation was that there was little discussion about my development – it was understood that I would take any initiatives in this area. In the formal situation, a focus on development is usually built into the system, and therefore the manager is the one who takes the initiatives. The trouble is that the focus on measurement and pay can make open and meaningful discussion about development difficult. People are less likely to admit to weaknesses in their performance if they think this will affect their salary!

The nature of the system is generally a feature of the size of the organization. In my case, the degree of informality could only be sustained when the company was small: as it grew, more formal systems were perceived to be necessary. The bigger the organization, the more the system becomes a mechanism for collecting information and making complex decisions about pay; the greater the perceived need for objective measurement to provide consistency; and so the level of formality increases until the system becomes a fraught interruption of the day-to-day relationship between manager and subordinate rather than an organic part of it. Most managers find appraisals difficult because of this: *they are a formal interruption of the informal relationship*. Exercise 3.3 helps you to clarify the nature of the people management systems in your organization.

## EXERCISE 3.3

Spend a few minutes now reflecting on the performance management system in your organization. Use the five issues listed below to help you clarify the nature of the system:

- The level of formality.
- The link with pay.
- The emphasis on measurement.
- The value of subjectivity.
- The focus on development.

Now note down four ways in which the system affects the way you manage your people: these could be positive or negative.

### You and your organization

You may work in an organization where the values, policies and systems suit and support the way you want to manage. Or you may feel that they have been deliberately contrived to make your life as difficult as possible! Most managers will be somewhere in between these two extremes – and their effectiveness will be partly dependent on their ability to manage the organization's norms and requirements. Choices activity 3.1 gives you the opportunity to think about ways in which you can usefully assert yourself against the demands of your organization.

One of the choices that managers have is the extent to which they allow the values, policies and systems of their organization to dominate their management style. You can be active: trying to influence the values and managing the policies and systems in order to achieve your objectives. Or you can be passive: absorbing the values without question, implementing the policies and values without integrating them to the specific needs of your situation. For example, many managers see themselves as oppressed victims of the company appraisal system, powerless in the face of the implacable problems that it presents. But they often have far more freedom than they realize to find ways of using the system as a tool which will help them manage their people effectively. They let the system manage them when they should be managing the system.

## *CHOICES ACTIVITY 3.1*

Exercises 3.1, 3.2 and 3.3 have asked you to identify the ways in which your organization influences how you manage people. Activity 3.1 asks you to identify actions that you could take to manage your organization's values, policies or systems so that they do not disrupt the way you want to manage people.

Focus on three negative influences (you may have identified these through exercises 3.1, 3.2 and 3.3) and plan achievable and realistic actions that will improve your management of people.

Here are some examples to illustrate the kind of actions you might consider:

- I will not jump in with solutions when people come to me with problems. I will help them to find solutions for themselves.

- I will never send anybody on a training programme unless it is part of a broader development strategy.

- I will schedule regular meetings with people where we just discuss their performance.

## Summary

In the first section of this chapter we have looked at how the organization you work in can affect your choices about how to manage people. We have scratched the surface of a complex subject by exploring aspects of the organization's values, policies and systems. The purpose has been to help you to do the following:

- Be more aware of how you are influenced by the environment in which you work.

- Evaluate whether those influences are positive or negative.

- Identify actions which enable you to manage these influences so that they do not get in the way of you managing people effectively.

The next influencing factor we shall look at is the people themselves: what kind of people are they, and how does that affect the choices that you make as a manager?

# The People

In this section, we shall look at the people you manage and the ways in which they influence the choices you make about how you manage them. As 'people' is a vast subject area, we will focus on three factors that affect the practical everyday decisions that you make, as well as the kind of relationships that you establish. These are:

- Capability.
- Potential.
- Motivation.

## Capability

One of the key influences on how you manage people will be how good they are at doing their job. This seems simple enough, but like most people issues, is more complicated than it looks. For what it really means is: do they do the job as well as you want them to? There are two factors here: the standards that you apply in relation to the job; and the person's ability to achieve those standards of performance.

Your perception of people's ability will affect the way you manage their performance. You may feel that they exceed your expectations, meet them or fall below them. Each scenario is likely to produce a different response from you. But before evaluating their capability, it is worth reflecting on your standards, in order to assess their appropriateness. Case study 3.1 gives two examples from my own experience to illustrate potential problems.

## CASE STUDY 3.1

I once complained to a senior manager of a training consultancy I worked for that no attempt was being made to improve the training skills of its consultants. The manager patiently explained to me that, although the consultants might not be as good as I thought they should be, they were more than good enough to do the job they were employed to do: in fact, most of their customers commented on how much better they were than other trainers they had come across. I learnt that, in this case, my standards were not a good starting point for evaluating the capability of the consultants.

I was talking to a manager who was so dissatisfied with someone's performance that he was on the point of sacking him. The employee had complained that the manager's standards were unnecessarily high, that the customers did not require work of the quality that the manager was asking him to produce. This had caused the manager to doubt his own judgment. I asked him whether he would lower his standards even if the employee was right. His answer was: no, he wanted work of a particular standard, irrespective of the perceived requirements of the customer.

The stories in Case study 3.1 give conflicting messages. In the first scenario, I accepted that my standards were unrealistic and adjusted my expectations accordingly. In the other scenario, the manager's standards were integral to his vision for his department and so whether they were inappropriate or not was a non-issue: the manager was not prepared to adjust his expectations.

So capability is not just about how good people are. It is about how good they need to be and how good you want them to be. When judging the capability of your people, you need to first:

- Clarify in your own mind the standards to which you are expecting them to perform.
- Evaluate the appropriateness of those standards to the requirements of the job.
- Decide whether your *desired* standards override the *required* standards.

Exercise 3.4 asks you to use these steps to reflect on the nature of the standards you set your people.

## EXERCISE 3.4

Spend a few minutes now reflecting on the standards to which you expect your people to perform. Evaluate their appropriateness to the requirements of the job. Then decide whether your desired standards override the required standards.

| Capability level | Area: contribution | Objective |
|---|---|---|
| Low<br><br>↑<br><br>↓<br><br>High | Activity: management | • Ensure achievement of tasks and targets<br>• Develop confidence through achievement |
| | Performance: coaching | • Improve current performance and expand range of activity<br>• Develop new skills and capabilities |
| | Career: mentoring | • Delegate more tasks and responsibility<br>• Develop capability for next career stage |

**Figure 3.1** Areas of involvement and capability

When you have decided on the standards you want to operate by, you can assess people's performance in terms of their ability to achieve those standards. The level of their capability will be one of the factors that will determine what your contribution as a manager should be. This is illustrated in Figure 3.1.

## Potential

Having considered capability, the next issue is potential. There are two aspects to this. Do people have the potential to improve their performance to achieve the standards you have set – their short-term potential? Do they have potential to develop beyond their current jobs and into more valuable positions within the company – their long-term potential?

These questions will have a major influence on how you manage your people. They are also difficult questions to answer: a person's potential is very hard to assess. You can measure capability and you can assess results. But it is hard to anticipate how someone is likely to perform in the future. To a large extent, you have to trust your gut feeling: you usually know instinctively which of your people have got potential and which have not. You may be dreadfully wrong – some of your high-fliers may never take off. You may also be terribly unfair to someone who has potential that you just have not spotted. But in the end you should learn to trust your instincts, for the following two reasons:

- There is no rational method that I know of that can be guaranteed totally reliable. In most cases, methods tell you what your instincts have already put on file.
- If you do not feel instinctively that the potential is there, this will reduce your commitment and ability to help the person concerned to develop.

## EXERCISE 3.5

Spend a few minutes now reflecting on the short- and long-term potential of the people you manage.

- Using your subjective judgment, write their names down in the left-hand column of the table below in order of their potential (i.e. the person with the highest potential at the top of the list, etc.).
- Then write down reasons against each name to explain your judgment (e.g. bright, energetic, enthusiastic).

Name                          Reasons

- When you have filled in the table above, spend a few minutes reflecting on the extent to which you assess potential in terms of your personal strengths and preferences. For example, do you assess potential in terms of how methodical people are because you are a methodical person?

When you have used Exercise 3.5 to assess the potential of the people you manage, you can decide what your role as manager should be. Figure 3.2 shows how the level of potential relates to the required contribution from the manager.

## Motivation

The third characteristic of the people you manage that will affect the choices you make about them is their motivation: the level of

| Level of potential | Area: contribution | Objective |
|---|---|---|
| Low ↑ ... ↓ High | Activity: management | • Ensure capability to do current job<br>• Limit activity to protect team performance |
| | Performance: coaching | • Fulfil potential to do current job well<br>• Develop potential for next career stage |
| | Career: mentoring | • Fulfil potential to excel at current job<br>• Develop plan for medium-term career development |

**Figure 3.2** Areas of involvement and potential

energy, enthusiasm and commitment they bring to their work. If you feel that someone is highly motivated, your attitude to them is likely to be positive and generous, whatever their capability or potential. And vice versa: if somebody lacks commitment, however talented they are, your goodwill towards them will quickly erode.

There are many ways of understanding and labelling the forces that motivate people. They generally start from the premise that a person's motivation is based on a set of needs – the desire to achieve fulfilment of these needs is the force that motivates them. If people see work as an arena in which their needs can be fulfilled, they will be motivated to perform in ways that ensure their particular needs are met. If they do not see work as a viable arena, they will not be motivated and it will be hard to motivate them.

One way of defining needs is as drives for different kinds of recognition: we do things in order to get recognition and the kind of recognition we need will influence what it is that we do and how we do it. Dave Pellin suggested that there are three kinds of recognition that act as motivating forces. These are the need for:

- **Admiration:** When we are motivated by our vanity, our need to be admired by others.

- **Respect:** When we are motivated by our need for material reward and control.

- **Acceptance:** When we are motivated by our need to be liked and accepted by others.

Everyone has needs for all these kinds of recognition to some extent. Some people are clearly driven by one of them in particular, others by an equal measure of all three. You will probably know people whose behaviour is dominated by their need for admiration, for example. You will know others where it is hard to identify one need as being any more dominant than the others. And we change over time. When I was younger, I was driven almost exclusively by my need for admiration and applause. As I have become older, my need for respect has increased: although my vanity does not like to admit it, it does matter to me what car I drive!

Some people can obtain the recognition they need from the work that they do. This could take many forms: the need for admiration could be fulfilled by having a high-powered, high-profile position, or from being the one who makes everyone laugh on the shopfloor; the need for respect could be fulfilled by financial reward, or through having control over resources (school caretakers spring to mind!); the need for acceptance could be fulfilled by being part of a tight-knit working group, or by being the person that people turn to if they have got a problem.

Others cannot fulfil their needs for recognition through their work. They might feel they should have a more senior position (respect); or that they are not allowed to take any risks or initiatives of their own (admiration); or that they do not have enough contact with other people (acceptance). If this is the case, their motivation and commitment will suffer. They may lose interest in their work; they may become disillusioned or cynical; they may try to get their needs met in inappropriate ways – such as the manager who wants to be liked, or the joker who does not know when to stop.

Use Exercise 3.6 to consider how the need for recognition relates to the people you manage.

## EXERCISE 3.6

Spend a few minutes now reflecting on recognition as a motivating force.

- First, think about the people you manage: what kinds of recognition do they need, e.g. are they particularly motivated by the need for admiration, respect or affection, or by a combination of all of these?
- Second, think about the work that they do: does it provide them with enough of the recognition they need? Could it be organized to provide them with more of that recognition?

People's motivation suffers when they are not getting the recognition they need from the work that they do. So does their effectiveness. For example, there are ways in which my need for admiration is met by my work as a trainer: I am the centre of a group's attention for long periods. But if my need for applause is too dominant, it could make me insensitive – I will be using the group to feed my needs rather than helping them to meet their own. As I have become older, however, the level of fulfilment I achieve from being a trainer has decreased. I need applause of a different kind, from a bigger audience, and it is this need that motivates me to write this book.

Identifying people's needs in terms of recognition will help you to explore ways in which you can motivate them by giving them the recognition they need. Different kinds of recognition require different solutions:

- **Admiration:** the right kind of *activity* in the *arena* that will provide the required admiration and applause.

- **Respect:** the level of *responsibility*, *control* and *reward* that will satisfy the individual.

- **Acceptance:** the *roles* and *contact* with people from whom they can get the acceptance that they need.

It is not always easy to identify specific solutions, and even if you can, it is not always in your power to make them happen. You might not be able to provide somebody with the kind of responsibility they want – and you may not think they are capable of handling such a responsibility anyway. The extent to which you are able to meet people's needs for recognition will determine your choices about how you are going to manage people who lack motivation. Figure 3.3 shows how the level of motivation relates to the required contribution from the manager.

## Other factors

We have looked at people in three ways: their capability, their potential and their motivation. Each of these will affect the choices that you make about the way you manage your people as a group and as individuals. They will determine the extent to which you need to be a doer or developer; they will influence the extent to which you involve yourself in activity management and perform-

| Level of motivation | Area: contribution | Objective |
|---|---|---|
| Low ↑ ↓ High | Activity: management | • Ensure achievement of tasks and targets<br>• Increase motivation by meeting needs for recognition where possible<br>• Limit activity and responsibility to protect team performance |
| | Performance: coaching | • Sustain motivation by ensuring needs for recognition are being satisfied<br>• Develop job and performance to increase motivation |
| | Career: mentoring | • Ensure that aspiration is matched by potential<br>• Develop career plan that will satisfy future needs for recognition |

**Figure 3.3**  Areas of involvement and motivation

ance and career development. By focusing on these three factors, we have developed some rational processes by which you can reflect on the kind of people you manage and make decisions about how you do it.

These three factors are in different ways an expression of the individual's personality. There are other aspects of people's personality which will also affect your choices and decisions as a manager. There is not enough space to explore these other aspects in detail in this book. But before we move on, use Exercise 3.7 to help you to think about how the personalities of your people influence the way you manage them.

However hard we may try, it is inevitable that our decisions will be affected by our feelings about people. In fact, it is dangerous to pretend otherwise. If we try to *suppress* our subjective responses to people, we are only pushing them underground – they do not go away. They still affect our decisions, but subconsciously, so that we are less aware of their influence and therefore less able to control them. It is better to *manage* your subjective feelings, and to do this, you have to be honest with yourself: admitting that the feelings exist and acknowledging their power and influence.

## EXERCISE 3.7

Spend a few minutes now reflecting on the personalities of the people you manage:

- First, use five key words to describe the personality of each member of your team (e.g. aggressive, impatient, arrogant, creative, energetic, sensitive).

- Second, use five key words to describe your feelings about each of the personalities you have described (e.g. frustrated, intimidated, angry, competitive, impressed, pleased, relieved).

- Third, think of one instance for each person where your feelings about them has influenced a decision you have made (e.g. your frustration meant that you delegated work to someone else; your positive feelings meant that you did not confront a person on an issue of poor performance).

## You and your people

Choices activity 3.2 gives you the chance to do a subjective 'audit' of the group that you manage as the basis for evaluating the choices that you make about how you manage the group and the individuals within it.

The kind of people you manage will affect the decisions you make about how you relate to individuals and the group. Your completed table in Activity 3.2 may show that your people are very similar, in which case your decisions may focus on how you manage the group as a whole. If they are all very capable and highly motivated, for example, you may be best able to contribute by taking a low profile, co-ordinating their activity and developing performance where appropriate – a developer strategy. If their capability and motivation is low, you may have to ensure that the group meets its targets, managing activity as best you can to ensure that people develop confidence and enthusiasm – an enforced doer strategy.

On the other hand, your group may be made up of several very different personalities, some very capable, some not, some highly motivated, others uncommitted, some with high potential, some who will never progress further than where they are now. This is a more difficult scenario: with such a group, your choices will be about how to prioritize and focus your efforts to ensure that the group achieves its goals in a way that meets the needs of as many individuals as possible.

## CHOICES ACTIVITY 3.2

The table below provides you with a structure for 'auditing' your group in terms of the capabilities, potential and motivation of its members.

- First, write the names of each member of your group in the left-hand column of the table.

- Second, rank each person from 1–5 (5 being high) against each category. For example, if you think somebody has some potential, but not much, rank them 2. Use your subjective judgment initially, but then substantiate that judgment with a specific example in each case.

| Name | Capability | Potential | Motivation |
|------|------------|-----------|------------|
|  | 1 2 3 4 5 | 1 2 3 4 5 | 1 2 3 4 5 |
|  | 1 2 3 4 5 | 1 2 3 4 5 | 1 2 3 4 5 |
|  | 1 2 3 4 5 | 1 2 3 4 5 | 1 2 3 4 5 |
|  | 1 2 3 4 5 | 1 2 3 4 5 | 1 2 3 4 5 |
|  | 1 2 3 4 5 | 1 2 3 4 5 | 1 2 3 4 5 |
|  | 1 2 3 4 5 | 1 2 3 4 5 | 1 2 3 4 5 |

- Finally, use the table to review your relationships with each member of the group. Think about whether you are responding appropriately to their levels of capability, potential and motivation. If you feel that you are not, focus on one person and identify one step that you could take to manage that person more effectively.

## Summary

In the second section of this chapter we have looked at how the people you manage will be a major influence on the choices you make as a manager. We have focused on three criteria: capability, potential and motivation. Each is a complex issue in its own right and it is hard to make accurate and *objective* judgments about them. However, we make *subjective* judgments about them all the time. It is our responsibility as managers to monitor and control these subjective judgments so that they become a constructive basis for our decisions.

We will return to these three criteria when we look in detail at planning your contribution to managing and developing the performance of your people in Part 2, as they are important considerations when deciding where you should be investing your limited time and energy.

The next section of this chapter looks at the third and last of our influencing factors: you. It goes further into the issue of subjectivity by looking at the emotional bases for our choices and decisions as managers.

# You

Having said that the people you manage are complex, they are a feast of simplicity compared with you! You are the single biggest influence on the way you manage people. In this section, you are going to be exploring a few of the factors that make up the complex organism that is you and how those factors affect the way you manage the other complex organisms who work for you.

We shall focus on two aspects of you, which reflect and amplify issues explored earlier in this chapter. They are as follows:

- Values.
- Needs.

## Values

I used to have a colleague who had very strong views about things, a very clear sense of what was right and what was wrong: a very clear set of personal values. One of those was that people should work hard, which, for him, meant that they should work late, work at weekends, and never complain about having too much to do. This is what he did – he just criticized himself for not being organized enough to do it all (although he was actually highly organized). And he expected the same of the people he managed: for example, he became annoyed with them if they indicated that they would not work over a weekend to finish a report or proposal. He could not understand their attitude, he was highly critical, and this affected the way he saw them and, inevitably, the way he managed them.

You may feel that it was unreasonable of him to expect people to work at weekends, or you may feel that he was entirely justified. Values in themselves are not right or wrong. The problem was that he was imposing his values on people who did not share them and this was creating a tension in his team. He was not attempting to understand or respect the values of others – he was critical of them for being different from his.

Hard work is one example of a value that you may hold which affects your working relationships with the people you manage. You may believe that people's personal lives are more important than their work. You may believe that people should be honest, or that it is more important not to get found out. You may believe that people should take risks, or that people should only act when they are sure it is safe to do so. The list is endless. Some of our values will be definite decisions that we have made about how we want to be. Others will emerge less consciously, a reflection of our experiences and personalities.

Whatever our values are, the important thing is to understand how they affect the choices we make, and to ensure that they are not causing us to be rigid and intolerant. My colleague was 'dumping' his values on other people in a way that was oppressive and counterproductive. He needed to understand that his attitude to hard work was just that: *his* attitude, and not a universal law which should be obeyed by everybody. The rigidity of his belief was making it impossible for him to reach an accommodation with his team. Why should they respect his values when he did not respect theirs?

Use Exercise 3.8 to explore how your values influence the way you manage your people.

## EXERCISE 3.8

Spend a few minutes now reflecting on your personal values and the extent to which they influence your management of others.

- Identify five values that describe your attitudes and beliefs about your work (e.g. 'always be constructive').
- Think about one of the people you manage and consider the extent to which he or she shares each of these values.
- Consider how the similarity or difference between your values affects how you manage that person.

We all have sets of values that profoundly influence the way we manage ourselves and our relationships with others. We may be aware of some of these values, those which we regard as positive features of our personality; others may be so ingrained that we are unaware of them – they will only be apparent to the people around us. Obtaining feedback from colleagues or subordinates about their perception of your values can be a useful and revealing exercise.

Awareness of our values will help us to understand the basis for many of the decisions and actions that we take as managers. In particular, it will help us to understand areas of tension and conflict with the people we manage. We need to recognize what we *do* with our values: the extent to which we impose them on other people, or are prepared to accommodate their values and tolerate differences.

## Needs

In the previous section of this chapter, we explored the motivation of the people you manage in terms of their need for different kinds of recognition: admiration, respect and acceptance. In this section we shall look at your *own* needs for recognition and how they affect your choices as a manager.

Before we do this in detail, it is worth commenting briefly on the relationship between values and needs. Values are generally an externalization of your emotional needs. In most cases, they are a rationalization of those needs – a way of giving them a more objective substance and meaning. My colleague's values about hard work, for example, can be seen as simply his personal need to work hard. He wants recognition for being a hard worker (respect). But he is also 'projecting' that need on to his people – he wants them to need respect, because that validates his own need. Because they do not need to work hard, he loses respect for them.

When reflecting on your values, it is useful to see them in this way – as personal needs writ large – for this will help you to understand the differences between you and others. By seeing values as needs, you can stop yourself from assuming that your values are in some way superior. Your needs for recognition, and the extent to which these needs are met in the workplace, are at the heart of understanding the choices you make as a manager. Exercise 3.9 helps you to explore the relationship between your values and needs.

## EXERCISE 3.9

Spend a few minutes now reflecting on your values in terms of the need for different types of recognition. Focus on the five values that you considered in Exercise 3.8 and see if you can trace these back to an internal need for admiration, respect or acceptance (or a combination of the three).

Many managers are motivated primarily by the need for admiration: they are likely to be charismatic leaders, high energy, high profile, carrying people along with them by the force of their personality. In some circumstances this will be appropriate, in others it will not. At its worst, it can be destructive and demoralizing. The manager may be insensitive to the needs of the other members of the team, and possibly claim recognition that should be distributed more evenly within the team.

Many managers are motivated primarily by the need for respect: they tend to lead from behind, carefully evaluating their decisions and deploying the resources at their disposal. Again, sometimes this is appropriate and sometimes it is not. At its worst, it can be demotivating, as the manager's need for control and focus on resources can sap initiative and inspiration from the people they manage.

And there are many managers who are motivated primarily by the need for acceptance: they want to be liked by the people they manage, they do not want to offend or upset anyone. There are few situations where this is appropriate: if your main motivating force is the need for acceptance, it is unlikely that that need will be met through being a manager and if you try to ensure that it is you are likely to cause problems either for yourself or for the people you manage. When people move into a management position for the first time, they can find the suddenness with which their need for acceptance and affection becomes inappropriate the hardest adjustment they have to make.

Our need for recognition influences our perceptions and our choices. My need for admiration, for example, meant that I saw my role as being the best trainer in the group of trainers that I managed, leading by example from that position and coaching and challenging people to improve their capability. The person who has replaced me is motivated far more by the need for respect: she is more interested in the effective deployment of the group's resources, a much more low-profile, control style of leadership.

When you do Exercise 3.10, you may be surprised by the closeness of the relationship between your choices and your needs. Decisions that we regard as rational or inevitable are often more likely to be the result of our own subjective preferences. These are so deep-rooted that the connection can be hard to see. But we rarely make decisions which are completely free from the influence of our needs for recognition.

The effectiveness of the choices you make will depend on the kind of leadership that is required of you by the organization and the

## EXERCISE 3.10

Spend a few minutes now reflecting on how your primary need for recognition (admiration, respect or acceptance) influences the choices you make as a manager. You may find it helpful to:

- Consider the options that exist in your own situation: what other choices could you have made?
- Compare the choices you make to those of other managers you know in similar positions to yourself.

specifics of your situation. In my example, the leadership requirement changed as the group matured: they did not need my energy and initiative any more – in fact, it had become inhibiting; what they needed was to consolidate and form their own identity. The emotional needs of myself and my successor were appropriate to the different situations that confronted us. But this is often not the case. If you have a high need for admiration and are working in a situation which does not require it, you are likely to be less than effective and less than happy. As we have seen in the earlier section on needs, if your need for recognition is not being met, your motivation will suffer.

The pressure which is generated when your needs are not being met may also distort your judgment and your behaviour. You may try to obtain the recognition you need in inappropriate ways: being too friendly with the people you manage; taking an irrationally tight hold over resources or control systems; trying to prove that you are better than any of the people you manage. To be effective, you need to do the following:

- Understand what your needs are.
- Recognize the extent to which they are being fulfilled.
- Be aware of how your choices and behaviour are affected if your needs are not being met.

Exercise 3.11 will help you to define the extent to which your job meets your needs, and the way that this influences your choices as manager. You may find this exercise hard to do. If you have struggled, or doubt whether your self-perceptions are accurate, you may find it helpful to ask someone whose opinion you trust for their feedback.

## EXERCISE 3.11

Spend a few minutes now reflecting on the extent to which your needs for recognition are met by your job as manager. In particular consider the extent to which:

- Your primary need for recognition is met by the specific nature of your situation (e.g. do you feel that you get the amount of respect that you need?).

- Your need for recognition, whether met or unmet, is leading you to make inappropriate or ineffective choices about the way you manage (e.g. does your need for respect lead you to not give others enough responsibility?).

## Other factors

We have looked at you and the kind of person you are in two ways: your values and your needs for recognition, and how these can influence the way you manage. There are other factors about you that will also influence the choices you make: aspects of your personality that we will not be covering in this book. We have not, for example, looked at how patient you are with people, or how comfortable you are at managing relationships, how shy or how assertive you are. In part, these traits will be an expression of your values and needs. But they are worthy of separate consideration, however brief. Exercise 3.12 asks you to do to yourself what you did to your people in Exercise 3.7: think about how your personality affects the people you manage.

## EXERCISE 3.12

Spend a few minutes now reflecting on your personality and the way it influences your choices as a people manager.

- First, use five key words to describe your personality (e.g. aggressive, impatient, arrogant, creative, energetic, sensitive).

- Second, use five key words to describe how your personality may affect one or more members of your team (e.g. frustrated, intimidated, angry, competitive, impressed, supported, trusting).

- Third, think of one instance when each aspect of your personality has affected the performance of one of your people (e.g. their fear of you has made them wary of taking initiatives).

The only way we can know for sure about how we affect other people is if they tell us, and this is something that does not happen that often at work. It requires a level of trust that is usually only experienced in close friendships and intimate relationships. Nor are we always that accurate with our perceptions of our own personality! We tend to have 'official stories' about who we are which are often far removed from how other people see us. You might be amazed to find out other people's perceptions and feelings about you.

So the exercise will only become really meaningful if you can get feedback from the people you manage about how they perceive your personality and how they feel it influences their work. Choices activity 3.3 will help you to think through how best to obtain that feedback if you feel that it would be useful to have it.

## *CHOICES ACTIVITY 3.3*

Plan how best you could get feedback from the members of your team about the way they perceive you as a manager and the way that your management style affects their performance and experience at work. You will need to make sure that the feedback is:

- Honest, but not destructive or hurtful.
- Detailed and specific enough for you to understand.
- Helpful to you in reviewing your own performance as a manager.
- Constructive enough to enable you to improve your performance as a manager.

You may feel that you are already clear about how the people you manage see you, that they give you honest and useful feedback regularly and that you do not need any more. On the other hand, you may feel that opening yourself up to them in this way is far too risky, too big a move away from the existing relationships that you have with your people. You may also feel that, given your situation or your style of management, such a move would be counter-productive, even positively dangerous. All of these may be true.

Asking for feedback about yourself in this way *is* risky, but it is also potentially extremely beneficial. The risks are that people may use the opportunity to vent their negative feelings about you in hurtful and destructive ways – feelings that may have more to do with who they are than with who you are. You may be asking for a level of openness that is inappropriate for the kind of group that you manage. Your people may feel suspicious of your motives or resentful about the nature of the demands that you are making.

The benefits are that you can learn how to manage yourself and your relationships with your people more effectively. This kind of feedback is potentially valuable information that can challenge your preconceptions about people, help you to understand their motives and responses, and most importantly, help you to coutrol and adapt your natural management and interactive style so that you are getting the best out of your people.

If you are to obtain these benefits, you need to minimize the risks by creating a safe environment in which people feel free to be open and honest with you, and in which you feel comfortable about receiving their feedback. This means that:

- They have to understand and trust your motives for asking for their feedback.

- They need to understand the nature of the feedback you are asking for and what you intend to do with it.

- You need to be able to hear and accept what people tell you without reacting defensively or challenging their perceptions.

- You need to monitor your internal responses to the feedback so that you do not reject valuable messages or overreact in ways that are not useful to you.

There are several ways in which you could obtain feedback about yourself as a manager. You could do it formally, through meetings with individuals or with the group as a whole. You could do it on paper, sending out a questionnaire about yourself and getting anonymous responses. You could have informal chats with your people over coffee or lunch. You could make it a feature of your annual appraisals or regular review meetings.

Planning how to get such feedback is an interesting exercise in itself and will tell you something about the choices you make. It will also help you think about your relationships with the people you manage, because it will pose questions like: how risky is it for them to be open with me? Is that a good thing or a bad thing? How do I feel about the prospect of receiving their feedback: curious, anxious, threatened? How complacent am I about my relationships with them? Do I know as much as I think I know?

## Summary

In the third and last section of this chapter we have looked at how who you are influences the choices you make as a manager. We have focused on two aspects: your values and needs. There are many other aspects that could have been explored. There are many tools that can be used to help you understand your personality and your preferences. I have focused on these two in order to help you explore the relationship between seemingly conscious and rational decisions and the unconscious and emotional processes from which they spring. Our choices are primarily an expression of our emotional make-up. They are none the worse for this. It is when we pretend that our decisions are purely rational that problems are more likely to occur. The purpose of this section has been to encourage you to reflect on how your emotional needs influence your choices and actions. The greater your understanding of this connection, the greater your ability to manage your subjective processes effectively.

# Part 2
## Planning

Part 2 helps you to organize the way you manage people. It gives you structures for planning your appraisals and your coaching activity. The activities in Part 2 give you the opportunity to use these structures to draw up your own appraisal and coaching plans.

# 4

# The performance management process

In Part 2, we shall be concentrating on how you organize the management of your people: the performance management process. In most cases, this will be divided into one-year blocks, which start and end with some form of annual appraisal and objective-setting meetings. During this year, your management of people will involve the following:

- **Planning:** Setting objectives, targets and standards to help people plan their activity for the year.

- **Doing:** Providing instructions and support to ensure that objectives are achieved to the required standard.

- **Reviewing:** Monitoring, assessing and measuring performance to check whether objectives have been achieved and to decide rewards.

This **pla.. do–review** cycle is the basic process of people management. It operates at two levels:

- The macro level – the management of the year's activity.
- The micro level – the development of performance through involvement at the **doing** stage.

This is illustrated in Figure 4.1:
We shall be working through the process of both the cycles in Figure 4.1 in detail. In Chapter 5, we shall focus on the annual

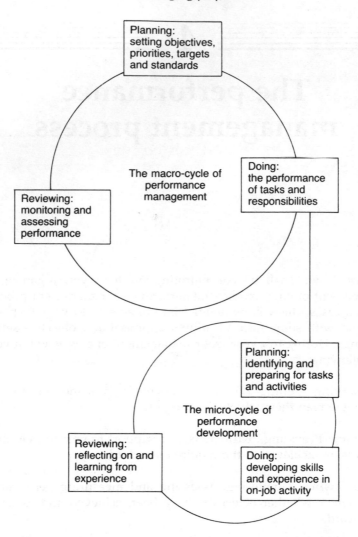

**Figure 4.1** The macro-cycle of performance management

appraisal, which is usually when most of the planning and review-ing at the macro level takes place. In Chapter 6, we shall focus on planning your coaching activity. Before we move on to these specifics, however, this chapter will explore two broad issues which relate to both levels of the people management process. These are your overall objectives, and your on-going process.

Throughout Part 2, the emphasis will be on being **proactive** as a people manager. Each chapter asks you to make conscious decisions about your objectives, strategies and activity with regard to each of the people you manage. If you do the activities, you will have planned your contribution for the year ahead. You will also have worked through some of the key decisions that you need to take if you are to resist the pressure to manage reactively.

# Overall objectives

Like any management activity, people management needs to be driven by clear and realistic objectives. You will be able to manage your people effectively if you have an objective for each individual which defines where you want that person to be at the end of the year, an objective which is superordinate to the specific goals and targets that have been agreed. Here are some examples of overall objectives:

- Get Susan to take over the auditing work.
- Get Jean ready for promotion next year.
- Get Rachel to communicate effectively with users.
- Make sure Peter is able to sell to big prospects on his own.
- Get Ron to face up to the fact that he does not have the potential to become a manager.
- Make sure Jack is taking more initiative to anticipate problems.

Objectives such as these become the driver which shapes how you manage at the macro level, and the extent to which you become involved at the micro level. Some managers have a clear idea of their overall objectives for each of their people. Others are less sure: they may have a rough idea of what they want to achieve, but no clearly defined superordinate objective which is the starting point for the decisions they make about how to manage each person. Exercise 4.1 will help you to decide how clear you are.

## EXERCISE 4.1

Spend a few minutes now reflecting on how clear you are about your overall objective for each of the people you manage.

# Levels of objective

In the list of examples that I gave above, there were different kinds of objective. These related to three of the levels of involvement explored in Chapter 2, as shown in Figure 4.2. The first step is to decide which level of overall objective is appropriate for your people. This will depend on the level of each person's capability, potential and motivation, as we have seen in Chapter 3. Figure 4.3 illustrates this with an example of how a manager has rated one of her people against these criteria. In Figure 4.3, the person was doing his current job reasonably well and enthusiastically but, in the manager's opinion, he did not have the potential to improve his current level of performance. Because of his low potential, the appropriate level for the overall objective was at the **activity** level, directed at increasing the volume of work without impairing standards.

The table can be used as an assessment-mapping tool which will help you clarify your assesment of people and identify the appropriate level of overall objective. As you use the tool, you may have to clarify the meaning of each criteria for different people. For example, motivation could mean motivation to do the current job, to improve performance or to develop a career; similarly, potential could be the potential to improve in the short term, or to go far in the long term.

| Objective | Definition | Example |
|---|---|---|
| Activity | Objectives which state the range and kind of activity you want the person to be able to do by the end of the year | Get Susan to take over the auditing work<br>Make sure Peter is able to sell to big prospects on his own |
| Performance | Objectives which state the improvements that you want to see in the person's performance by the end of the year | Get Rachel to interact effectively with users<br>Make sure Jack is taking more initiative to anticipate problems |
| Career | Objectives which state the steps that need to be taken by the end of the year to develop the person's career appropriately | Get Jean ready for promotion next year<br>Get Ron to face up to the fact that he hasn't got the potential to become a manager |

**Figure 4.2** The three levels of overall objective

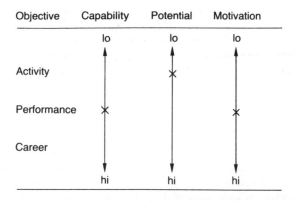

**Figure 4.3** Identifying the appropriate level (of overall objective)

The tool can produce a number of variations which reflect the large number of possible scenarios. It will not always be easy to be sure about what level of overall objective is best. Here are some examples which may be of help.

**Activity** objectives would be appropriate for people who are:

- New to the job and/or have little experience in the activities involved (low capability).
- Doing the job adequately but have no potential to improve (low potential).
- Good performers who want to stay in the same job and not progress their career (low motivation, i.e. not motivated to move on).

**Performance** objectives would be appropriate for people who are:

- Not performing as well as you would like and have the potential to improve (low capability/medium potential).
- Performing well and have the potential to take on new areas of work or greater responsibilities (high potential).
- Keen to improve their performance or career and have the potential to do so (high motivation/medium potential).

**Career** objectives would be appropriate for people who are:

- Performing badly and have no potential to improve (low capability/low potential).

- High performers who have the potential to further their career in the organization (high potential).
- Good performers who will become frustrated if their career does not progress soon (high motivation).

Planning activity 4.1 will help you to assess your people.

## PLANNING ACTIVITY 4.1: ASSESSMENT MAPPING

Use Figure 4.3 as a tool to map your assessment of one of the people you manage in terms of their capability, potential and motivation.

- Copy the table (minus the crosses!) on to a separate sheet of paper, and mark where you rate each person on the three vertical lines.
- Then decide, given your ratings, which level of overall objective is appropriate for that person: activity, performance or career.

Selecting the right level of overall objective at the beginning of the year is of fundamental importance. Problems are often caused by managers unconsciously choosing the wrong level. Case Study 4.1 gives two contrasting examples of this.

## CASE STUDY 4.1

John had been investing a lot of time in coaching one of his salespeople, Frank, to try and persuade him to be more flexible when dealing with customers, to be less task driven and abrasive. Frank was a successful salesman, one of John's top performers, and was also highly motivated both to perform well and to further his career. But he did not have the potential to improve. He was set in his ways to such an extent that he did not accept there was a problem, let alone that he needed to do something about it. John was getting nowhere. It became clear that John had set a *performance* objective instead of an *activity* objective. Rather than invest time in trying to improve Frank's skills, he should have managed his activity to make sure that he kept bringing in the figures and did not offend any major customers in the process.

Kurt had delegated to Sonia a major software system implementation in the USA. He knew from previous experience that Sonia was not good at getting buy-in from people, but she was technically excellent and so the best person to do the job. Because he had not established a clear performance objective, however, the targets he set Sonia just reflected **what** he wanted her to do rather than **how** he wanted her to do it. Her target was to get the system up and running by a certain date. To reflect an overall performance objective, the target should have been to *get buy-in from all users to the new system* by a certain date. This would have ensured that she would be measured on the how, not just the what, and would have forced her to consider the way she interacted with users.

In each example in the case study, changing the level of overall objective was the first step in redirecting the manager's strategy and effort. The next step was to clarify what the overall objective should be, as follows:

- John's **activity** objective should be to maintain Frank's good sales performance and make sure he does not offend any major customers.

- Kurt's **performance** objective should be to improve Sonia's ability to interact effectively with colleagues and internal customers.

Objectives such as these provide the starting-point for defining what kind of contribution from the manager would be most appropriate. They are also the starting-point for defining specific objectives and targets to ensure that the criteria by which people's performance will be measured at the end of the year reflect the manager's overall objectives.

When defining your overall objective for each of your people, there are three points that you should bear in mind. Your objectives should be:

- **Realistic:** It is important that the objectives you set yourself for the people you manage are realistic – ones that you will be able to achieve. It is tempting to set targets which are too big or too challenging, which ask the person to move too far, too fast. It is also tempting to either underestimate the amount of support they will need from you if the objective is to be achieved, or overestimate the amount of time you will be able to give them. You should make sure that your overall objective not only reflects the individual's capability, potential and motivation, but also the amount and nature of the support that will be available. I know several managers who, for positive reasons, tend to be overambitious and who cause themselves and their people frustration and disappointment as a result.

- **Honest:** It is likely that most of the people you manage will have a generally high level of capability, potential and motivation. But there may be some for whom this is not the case: people who are never going to be good enough, who have aspirations beyond their potential, who have problems with their attitude that are seriously affecting their performance and so on. It can be difficult to set useful overall objectives for these people and we often back off from confronting the issue. This may be because we hope things will improve or because we fear the consequences if we tackle the issue head on. Unfortunately, things rarely improve of their own accord, and the consequences tend to get worse the longer the issue is allowed to continue. It is important that your overall objectives honestly reflect your assessment of individuals. I know many managers who have not been ruthless enough in setting their objectives. They generally know what needs to happen, but are avoiding facing the issue.

- **Balanced:** If you manage more than one person, you will have to balance your overall objectives for each individual in order to make sure that you achieve your group objectives. The balance will depend on circumstances: the requirements of the work, the nature of the people and the scope for advancement within the organization. There may be times when the objective you want to set for an individual has to be moderated to meet the needs of the group. For example, you might have to hold back a high-flier for a year while you develop her replacement within the team. You might have to be more ruthless than you would like to be with a low performer because he is affecting the morale of the rest of the group.

## PLANNING ACTIVITY 4.2: OVERALL OBJECTIVES

Plan your overall objective for each of the people you manage. These objectives could be for the year starting from today. Or you could set them for the period of time that best suits your needs. You should use the following steps:

1. Use the assessment mapping tool on each person to identify the appropriate level of overall objective: activity, performance or career.

2. Write down an overall objective for each person, according to the level that you have identified, which defines what you want to have achieved with that person by the end of the year.

3. Review these individual objectives to ensure that they meet the needs of the team, and revise any if necessary.

Planning activity 4.2 will help you to clarify your thinking about what you want to achieve with the people you manage. I trust that you will be ruthlessly honest with yourself, and set objectives which both reflect your real perception of the capability, potential and motivation of your people, and ones which you have a realistic chance of achieving.

---

# Goal setting

---

The overall objectives that you have set in Planning activity 4.2 will provide the springboard for the *specific* objectives or goals that you agree with your people to determine their activity for the coming year. The people-management system in your organization may include a formal goal-setting process, giving you guidelines for how these goals should be decided. It may be that there is no formal system, but an expectation that you will set goals for your people at the beginning of the year. If you work in a small organization, there may be no goal-setting process at all – just a shared understanding of what needs to happen.

In my experience, there are two problems with formal or semi-formal goal-setting processes. These are as follows:

- They are not based on a clear overall objective for the individual which provides a context for their specific goals.
- Partly as a result of this, they tend to generate activity-based goals, which can fail to state explicitly the element of perform-ance improvement required for the goal to be achieved satisfac-torily.

The focus on activity is appropriate if the overall objective is at the activity level. The goal will specify what is to be done and provide criteria for measuring its accomplishment. It is less useful if the overall objective is at the performance or career level, because if you only specify the activity, you will not clarify expectations or provide a suitable base for monitoring and measuring performance.

In case study 4.1, we saw how Kurt redefined his goal for Sonia so that it reflected his performance objective for her – to persuade her to improve her interaction with people. His original activity-level target allowed her to continue to think that her priority was the task rather than the process and so avoid facing the issue about her poor communication skills. The new target retained the core activity but added the performance element, to leave Sonia in no doubt about what was expected of her and how her performance was going to be measured.

## EXERCISE 4.2

> If you set specific goals or objectives for your people at the beginning of the working year, spend a few minutes now reflecting on whether these goals focus only on activity, or whether they reflect the change or improvement in performance that you want the person to make.

If your overall objective for somebody is at the performance or career level, their specific objectives or targets should reflect this, in order to establish clear expectations and criteria for measuring performance which support what you are trying to achieve. There are two questions to ask yourself which will help you to turn activity goals into performance goals. They are:

- Why do I want them to do it?
- What will stop them doing it well?

Case study 4.2 gives two examples from a recent workshop which illustrate how these questions can help. After you have read the case study carry out Planning activity 4.3.

## CASE STUDY 4.2

One of the goals Hans had set Michel was: to write guidelines for using the employee payroll system by the end of July. This is a reasonable activity goal, but Hans wanted to turn it into a performance goal. He asked himself the two questions:

- Why? So that other people could use the payroll system when Michel was not available.
- What will stop him doing it well? He is not good at writing things clearly so that other people can understand and apply them.

The answers to the questions helped Hans to formulate a performance-focused goal, which was **to enable other people to imple-**

**ment the employee payroll system by producing guidelines by the end of July which are clear and easy to apply.**

Carol has set Johann this activity goal: to co-ordinate the activity of the various Quality Improvement groups on the site. To turn this into a performance goal, Carol asked herself the two questions:

- Why? To ensure consistency and avoid duplication.
- What will stop him doing it well? Johann is not good at spending time with the groups and communicating with them assertively.

The answers to the questions helped Carol to formulate a performance-focused goal, which was **to communicate regularly and effectively with the Quality Improvement groups to ensure a consistency of approach and to avoid duplication of effort.**

## PLANNING ACTIVITY 4.3: GOAL SETTING

Write specific goals for one of your people for whom you set an overall objective at the performance level, i.e. write performance-focused goals for them. If you have already written goals or objectives for this person, you should first review the goals you have set and, if necessary, rewrite them so that they focus on performance.

If your organization emphasizes the need for measurable goals, you may have found it difficult to write performance-focused goals that conformed to this criterion. It can be hard to measure effective performance because this can often be dependent on the responses of other people. Johann's ability to communicate effectively, for example, may be limited by the hostility of the Quality Improvement groups towards any kind of central control. Sometimes it is impossible to identify meaningful measures which will help you to assess someone's performance.

Wherever possible, your goals should be measurable as this will make the job of monitoring progress easier. There are appraisal systems which use complex goal-setting processes, incorporating the use of targets and standards in order to instil a level of objectivity into the measuring of performance. The danger is that these processes are applied so rigidly that the effort required is disproportionate to the value gained. Goals, targets and standards are only useful if they are meaningful to both parties. If you start to get bogged down when you try to write them, check whether the process is overriding the function! The purpose of setting goals is to

*Managing people*

help you clarify your expectations and measure whether they have been achieved. Sometimes the clarification is more important than the measurement. Like all tools, make sure they are working for you, rather than the other way round.

# Objectives and processes

Once you have established your overall objectives and set your specific objectives or goals, the next step is to identify the **process** you need in order to achieve these objectives. 'Process' here refers to the frequency and nature of the contact you have with each person. This will partly be determined by your circumstances: you may work alongside your people, in the same office for example, and so have constant access to them; on the other hand, they may work on a different site, even in a different country, in which case your contact will be much less frequent.

The process will also be determined by the management policies and systems of your organization. These usually require you to make formal contact at least once a year with your people at the annual appraisal; sometimes they provide a structure for formal or semi-formal contact throughout the year, insisting that you have quarterly reviews for example. Such events are attempts to ensure that you carry out the various functions involved in managing people. It is likely that you will be expected to do some, if not all, of the following:

- Set objectives and targets for the people you manage
- Monitor the achievement of these targets.
- Make decisions or recommendations regarding pay and rewards.
- Review performances and identify ways of improving them.
- Devise performance and career development plans and pass these on to a central personnel function.
- Review and improve the relationship between you and each of your subordinates.

In many organizations, most of these functions tend to be carried out at the annual appraisal, which becomes the focal point for the formal aspects of people management.

# The problems with appraisals

The problem with most appraisal systems is that by their very nature they tend to collect all the functions of people management into one key activity: the appraisal interview. This creates three kinds of difficulty for the manager:

- **Overload:** Most appraisals suffer because the manager is under pressure to gather and record an enormous amount of sophisticated information in a short space of time.

- **Conflict:** Some of the required functions conflict with each other. The need to make decisions about pay can overshadow all other functions, for example, especially in the mind of the appraisees, who may often be unwilling to discuss any other issue openly until they know how you are going to rank, rate, grade or scale them (or until they have persuaded you that your decision is wrong!).

- **Rigidity:** The formality of the system makes the interaction between manager and subordinate rigid and unnatural. The need to fulfil the system's requirements means that the manager can lose sight of the needs and feelings of the individual being appraised. Several managers, for example, have complained to me about having to go through the motions of discussing career development with people who have no desire to develop their career whatsoever.

It is because of these three difficulties that most people, managers and appraisees alike, do not like appraisals. In some of the companies I have worked with, people have dreaded them. In others, they have been dismissed as a complete waste of time. At best they are seen as a necessary evil that hinders rather than helps the real business of managing people. I have never yet come across an appraisal system which has been universally liked, welcomed and admired by managers!

Appraisals will always be difficult because one of their functions is to make decisions about pay and rewards. These decisions are confronting: they force you to evaluate people, compare them, make distinctions, decide that some people are more valuable than others and tell the others that they are less valuable. But you can make appraisal time more bearable by seeing the appraisal as a tool for helping you to achieve your objectives, rather than an obligation imposed on you by the personnel department. You need to incorporate it into your process for managing people, rather than see it as an interruption of that process.

One way of doing this is to decide how many functions *have* to be carried out at appraisal time. This will vary from company to company, depending on their administrative processes, but it is often the case that many of the functions that you *assume* have to be done at the appraisal can be done at other times in the year. For example, you could discuss career development with your people whenever you like, formally or informally or you could have regular meetings to review performance throughout the year, so that the appraisal becomes a convenient mechanism for summarizing what has been discussed.

It may be that all that you actually *have* to do at the appraisal itself is submit your recommendations about pay, or fill in the documentation to satisfy the personnel department. The other functions can be carried out as part of your on-going process of people management. Use Exercise 4.3 to consider the appraisal system in your organization.

## EXERCISE 4.3

If your company operates a formal appraisal system, spend a few minutes now reflecting on the various functions that the system is intended to achieve:

- First, consider whether there are any functions you need to add to or remove from the list given in the text (page 72).
- Second, consider how many of those functions actually have to be completed at the appraisal itself; could they be carried out at other times in the year?

# The on-going process

Most managers know that managing people is an on-going process: it does not just happen at the appraisal, it is an all-the-year-round activity. The trouble is that, for many managers, their on-going process is the informal, day-to-day relationship that they have with their people. And this does not necessarily mean that they are proactively managing the various functions listed earlier, or that they have a coherent strategy for achieving their overall objectives. In fact, these broader concerns are often swamped in the daily grind of short-term issues, needs and details. In reality, the informal, day-to-day relationship is usually mainly concerned with activity management.

We shall now look at establishing a **proactive** on-going process so that, throughout the year, you are actively managing all the functions that need to be managed in order to achieve the overall objectives that you have set. In such a process, the appraisal interview becomes one of several milestones which has a specific role, usually to do with documenting information that has been gathered earlier and making decisions about pay. The on-going process is designed to ensure that all the functions are covered without undue overload, conflict or rigidity.

The process you establish should be driven by your overall objective for each person. This will determine the following three things:

- **Frequency:** How often you need to meet: do you need to meet once a week, once a month, once a quarter?

- **Function:** The purpose for the meetings: for example, is the function to monitor progress, or to develop performance?

- **Formality:** The level of formality required: for example, do you agree a time in advance, agree an agenda and take notes, or do you have a chat over lunch in the canteen?

For example, if your objective is to:

- Make sure Peter is able to sell to big prospects on his own, the process may involve some formal coaching sessions where you go on sales calls together, followed by a series of semi-formal monthly meetings for the first half of the year to review his progress and give feedback and support. As he becomes more confident, you could move to a quarterly review in order to regularly assess his performance.
- Get Rachel to communicate effectively with users, you may decide that the best process would be to meet with her soon informally to give her some hard feedback about the way she manages her contact with users at the moment. If this does not

have any impact, you could have another, formal meeting with her to set measurable targets followed by regular formal meetings to review progress.

- Get Jean ready for promotion next year, you may want to give her increasing responsibility and freedom to get her used to being a supervisor. Your process may involve quarterly semi-formal meetings to review how she is getting on and make sure that she is learning from experience. You may also want to have as much informal contact as you can to ensure that she is being successful in order to develop her self-confidence – you might try to have lunch with her once a week.

It is likely that each of your people will require a different process. This will depend partly on your overall objective for them, and partly on their needs and personality. Some people like to have frequent contact and receive close support; others prefer to be left to get on with things and regard support as interference. We will look at these different preferences in more detail in Chapter 6.

The process you identify should take some of the pressure off of the annual appraisal. The most obvious way to do this is to have formal or semi-formal reviews two or three times a year in which you assess people's performance against their specific objectives in order to:

- Recognize and consolidate successes.
- identify any problems, difficulties or shortfalls.
- Give them feedback about their performance.
- Plan strategies for improving performance in the next period.

This will ensure that issues are dealt with as they arise, rather than being left to the end of the year. It will also give people the opportunity to take steps to improve their performance in line with your expectations. Planning activity 4.4 will help you devise such on-going processes.

The on-going process can take many forms, and will depend on the specific nature of your organization, the work that you do and the people that you manage. Some companies insist on quarterly meetings which are semi-formal reviews of targets and standards of performance. Other companies have appraisal systems in two stages, separating a review of past activity to make decisions about pay from a discussion about performance and career development. Some managers involve their subordinates in deciding what the best

## PLANNING ACTIVITY 4.4: THE ON-GOING PROCESS

Plan the best on-going process for each of the people you manage. This process should help you to achieve:

- Your overall objective for each person.
- The people-management functions that you identified in Exercise 4.2.

Decide for each person:

- How often you need to meet.
- What the functions of your meetings should be: to monitor activity or review performance.
- How formal the meeting should be.

process will be, setting up individual 'contracts' which govern their working relationship through the year.

You may feel that the way you manage your staff now is perfectly adequate to achieve all the functions required of you. Or you may feel, especially if you manage a lot of people, that you do not have enough time for the appraisal interviews, let alone any other meetings. At the least, I hope you have found it useful to think about how best to separate the various functions so that you do not overload the appraisal interview. At best, I hope you have devised a proactive and realistic process to ensure that you have the right amount and kind of contact to get the best out of all the people you manage.

# Summary

In this first chapter of Part 2, you have been asked to do two things:

- Set an **overall objective** for each of the people that you manage. These objectives are the drivers of the processes and strategies you will develop for effectively managing the individual members of your team.
- Plan the **on-going process** which you will use to structure your contact with each of the people you manage. This process is a series of meetings through the year, varying in frequency,

formality and function. The process involves the proactive management of your working relationship with each person; it includes the proactive management of the appraisal system so that you are using it as a tool to meet your needs and objectives.

In the following chapters of Part 2, we will look in more detail at the strategies required to achieve your objectives. These may involve you in revisiting, and possibly changing the objectives and processes you have identified in this chapter, as you explore relevant issues in more detail. This is likely to happen in reality anyway, as the year progresses and people and circumstances change in that bewildering and unexpected way that is becoming an increasing feature of our lives.

The next chapter looks specifically at planning for appraisal interviews. The lessons it contains, however, are not just relevant to appraisals: they can be applied throughout the year, as part of your on-going process.

# 5

# Planning appraisals

In this chapter, we shall look at how to plan effectively for appraisal interviews. The planning structure that I shall suggest has evolved through my experience of helping several companies implement their appraisal systems effectively. It will help you to use the appraisal as a tool for achieving your people-management objectives.

The structure focuses on planning how to tackle particular aspects of the appraisal interview. These are as follows:

- Reviewing the achievement of activities and targets.
- Reviewing standards of performance.
- Identifying targets and activities for the next period.
- Identifying required improvements in performance.
- Planning strategies and actions for achieving the targets, activities and improvements in performance that have been identified.

Although this does not cover every function that may be required of you by your appraisal system, it does cover the aspects of the appraisal that take up the most time and are often the most difficult to handle. They are also the aspects you are likely to address throughout the year as part of your on-going process.

The planning structure is divided into five stages:

1. Preparing the agenda.
2. Identifying outcomes.

3. Diagnosing performance problems.
4. Planning solutions.
5. Creating the appropriate climate.

The activities in this chapter will enable you to plan the appraisal of one of the people you manage. You should decide **now** who that person is going to be. Ideally it should be someone who:

- Does work that is similar to most of the other people you manage.
- Is an average performer – someone who performs adequately but who has areas where improvement is necessary.
- You relate to reasonably well – not your biggest problem, nor your oldest friend.

# Preparing the agenda

The first stage in the planning process is to decide which issues you want to discuss when reviewing the appraisee's performance, and in what order you are going to tackle them. This will be based on the following:

- The person's job.
- The objectives that you want to achieve.
- The issues that need tackling.

## Key job factors

Your appraisal system may already provide you with a way of breaking your appraisee's job down into a series of areas. These may be called job factors, job segments, key effectiveness areas or some other fragrant example of human resources-speak! In my experience, however, many of the appraisal systems which are based on such a breakdown tend to define jobs in terms of *activities* rather than *performance areas*, which means that some aspects of performance can be left off the list, such as managing relationships or taking initiative; and these are often the aspects where the problems occur and which are the hardest for appraisers to deal with.

Planning activity 5.1 asks you to write down the key job factors for the person you have decided to use as the basis for the planning activities in this chapter. The key job factors are the elements of the job that are integral to its effectiveness. This may be: an area of activity, or a requirement of the job.

For example, if the person is a computer hardware salesman, his key job factors might be as follows:

- Planning – strategy, activity, sales calls.
- Selling new business.
- Selling add-on business.
- Account management.
- Administration.
- Time management/organization.
- Customer relationships.
- Internal relationships (customer services/post-sales support).
- Teamwork.

This is a combination of measurable activities and other, less tangible aspects of the job that may affect the performance of the salesman or some of his colleagues.

## PLANNING ACTIVITY 5.1: KEY JOB FACTORS

Identify the key job factors for your chosen appraisee. For ease of management, there should be no more than ten factors, so do not break the job down into too much detail. Write the key job factors down, in any order, in a column on the left hand side of a piece of A4 paper. Keep this handy as you will be referring to it and adding to it throughout this chapter.

## Ranking importance

This list of key job factors written down during Planning activity 5.1 provides you with the basis for your agenda. You now need to decide whether to discuss all of these topics during the appraisal and in what order to sequence the topics you do want to discuss.

The next step will help you to do this by getting you to weight your key job factors in terms of their relative importance to each other. Their importance should be determined by your objectives as a manager. If, for example, you want your salespeople to concen-

| Key job factors | | | Importance | | |
|---|---|---|---|---|---|
| Planning | 1 | 2 | 3 | ④ | 5 |
| Selling new business | 1 | 2 | ③ | 4 | 5 |
| Selling add-on business | 1 | 2 | 3 | 4 | ⑤ |
| Account management | 1 | 2 | 3 | 4 | ⑤ |
| Administration | 1 | 2 | ③ | 4 | 5 |
| Time management | 1 | 2 | 3 | ④ | 5 |
| Customer relationships | 1 | 2 | 3 | 4 | ⑤ |
| Internal relationships | 1 | 2 | 3 | ④ | 5 |
| Teamwork | 1 | ② | 3 | 4 | 5 |

**Figure 5.1**  Key job factors: importance ranking

trate their efforts this year on getting more business from existing customers, this will be more important to you than selling new business. Figure 5.1 shows the importance ranking for the salesman's key job factors (1 = low importance and 5 = critical importance).

Ranking the key job factors in this way, as you are asked to do in Planning activity 5.2, will help you to clarify what your priorities are. In conjunction with the next planning step (5.3) it will provide you with an at-a-glance map of your person's performance.

## PLANNING ACTIVITY 5.2: IMPORTANCE RANKING

Rank the key job factors you identified in the previous activity on a 1–5 scale in terms of their importance to you as a manager (1 = low, 5 = high). Write your rankings down against your key job factors as shown in Figure 5.1, leaving space for a further column to be added in the next activity.

Some managers object that all their key job factors are equally important, and rank them all 4 or 5. Sometimes this is genuinely the case, but more often it stems from a reluctance to admit that any aspect of the job could be unimportant. Your importance ranking should reflect *your* priorities as a manager – even if these differ from what the organization *says* your priorities should be. If you feel you have been too conservative, redo the activity so that the rankings represent the weightings you actually *apply* at work.

# Ranking Effectiveness

Having mapped out your key job factors and their relative weighting, the next step is to rank the effectiveness of the person's performance with regard to each element of their job. At this stage, your ranking should be two things:

- Entirely subjective – you should delve into your gut and wallow in the bubbling jacuzzi of subjectivity that you will find there!

- Ruthlessly honest – you should stick with your instinctive assessment; do not drift toward the middle numbers because they are less controversial. Your ranking should reflect what you *really* think about their performance.

## *PLANNING ACTIVITY 5.3: EFFECTIVENESS RANKING*

Rank the key job factors you identified in the previous activity on a 1–5 scale in terms of the effectiveness of the appraisee's performance (1 = poor, 5 = high). Write your effectiveness rankings down in a column to the right of your importance rankings against the appropriate key job factors.

When you have done Planning activity 5.3, you will have completed your at-a-glance map which provides you with an overview of the person's performance. Although this overview is subjective, it will help you to identify the objective data you will need to gather in preparation for the appraisal to back up your subjective judgments. You may already have some 'hard evidence'; you may be able to collect data before the appraisal; or there may be issues for which objective data does not exist. It may be hard, for example, to obtain data which back up your judgment that the salesman is not a good team-player. The absence of hard evidence does not invalidate your subjective judgment, although it may be useful to check out whether other people share your perceptions of the issue.

The map also provides you with the information you need to plan the agenda for the appraisal interview. We will explore the potential of this information by using the example of the salesman. Figure 5.2 shows his finished map, including the effectiveness ranking.

| Key job factors | Importance | | | | | Effectiveness | | | | |
|---|---|---|---|---|---|---|---|---|---|---|
| Planning | 1 | 2 | 3 | ④ | 5 | 1 | 2 | ③ | 4 | 5 |
| Selling new business | 1 | 2 | ③ | 4 | 5 | 1 | 2 | 3 | 4 | ⑤ |
| Selling add-on business | 1 | 2 | 3 | 4 | ⑤ | 1 | 2 | ③ | 4 | 5 |
| Account management | 1 | 2 | 3 | 4 | ⑤ | 1 | 2 | 3 | ④ | 5 |
| Administration | 1 | 2 | ③ | 4 | 5 | 1 | ② | 3 | 4 | 5 |
| Time management | 1 | 2 | 3 | ④ | 5 | 1 | ② | 3 | 4 | 5 |
| Customer relationships | 1 | 2 | 3 | 4 | ⑤ | 1 | 2 | 3 | 4 | ⑤ |
| Internal relationships | 1 | 2 | 3 | ④ | 5 | 1 | ② | 3 | 4 | 5 |
| Teamwork | ① | 2 | 3 | 4 | 5 | ① | 2 | 3 | 4 | 5 |

**Figure 5.2** Key job factors: effectiveness ranking

## Interpreting the map

### EXERCISE 5.1

Spend a few minutes now reflecting on the information that the salesman's map provides by answering the following questions:

- What areas of his performance would you concentrate on during the appraisal interview?
- Are there any aspects of his performance that you think would be discussed more appropriately outside of the appraisal interview?

The salesman's map illustrates several types of issue:

- Areas of high importance where the salesman is under-performing, such as selling add-on business and internal relationships.
- Areas where the effectiveness exceeds the importance, such as selling new business.
- Areas of high importance where the salesman is performing well, such as customer relationships.
- Areas of low importance matched by low performance.

Given the manager's objectives, the main area to focus on is selling add-on business. There are a number of linked issues which need to be explored, account management and planning in particular. It will also be necessary to review the salesman's selling of new business, possibly in tandem with his time management.

There are two areas that could possibly be left alone: teamwork seems to be a non-issue for the manager, certainly not a priority. Administration, although more important to the manager than teamwork, is probably being performed at an adequate level: it may be best to ignore it in the appraisal to avoid overloading the salesman with criticism. The other area that it may be best to discuss outside the appraisal is the issue of internal relationships. This is likely to be a difficult issue and could take up a lot of time. Given that the priority is to shift activity from selling new business to optimizing existing accounts, it may be best to leave the internal relationships issue for a separate discussion, preferably before the appraisal interview.

## Ordering the agenda

Having decided what key job factors to discuss during the appraisal, the next step is to decide on how to order the agenda to provide the most constructive route for tackling the issues. Exercise 5.2 asks you to explore this, using the salesman's key job factors.

## *EXERCISE 5.2*

> Spend a few minutes now reflecting on the order in which you would discuss the key job factors if you were appraising the salesman in the example. Assume that administration, teamwork and internal relationships are being dealt with outside the appraisal interview.

There is no right answer to this exercise: there are several ways in which the agenda for the appraisal could be ordered effectively. However, there are four things that you need to consider.

The first is **climate**. Conventional wisdom has it that you should always start and end the appraisal on a positive note, focusing on areas of high performance. I am sceptical about this, for the following reasons:

- People are not fooled by it! Somebody once told me that he does not actually hear the positive feedback at the beginning because he is too busy trying to work out what the negative points will be later on!

- Although people like getting recognition, their positivity about the appraisal will be more affected by *how* you discuss things than by what you discuss. If you have not dealt with a poor performance area very well, the fact that you end the interview by discussing a positive one will not cut any ice at all! People will feel more positive about difficult areas that have been resolved to the satisfaction of both of you than about recognition for what they have done well.

- As we will see later, managers do not apply the same rigour to discussing good performance that they do to discussing poor performance. A few minutes at the beginning and end of an appraisal patting someone on the back will be totally overshadowed by two hours spent dissecting poor performance issues!

You do need to consider climate when you are ordering the agenda: you need to establish the climate that will best serve the objectives you want to achieve. For example, if you have got some tough issues to discuss, and the appraisee knows it, it may be best to get them on the table straight away rather than construct a 'positivity sandwich'.

The second issue that needs consideration is **momentum**. You will find it more useful to think of climate in terms of building up a positive momentum through the outcomes you achieve for each agenda item. If, for example, there are three areas where you want the appraisee to change or improve performance, start with the area where it will be easiest for you to obtain agreement to the changes you want. This will influence the climate of the discussion positively and provide a useful precedent for discussing the more difficult issues.

You also need to make sure that you deal with your **priority** issues in the time that you have made available. It may be risky, for example, to put your key issue low down on the agenda so that you have to rush it or run out of time. One the other hand, if you address it at the beginning, it could swallow up most of the available time and mean that you have to rush through the other issues on your agenda.

The most important thing to look for is **linkage** between issues. There are three reasons for this. Linking issues will help you to:

- Identify the best *strategic* route through the agenda.
- Avoid repetition and circular discussions as the same issues crop up in several agenda items.

- Use high performance areas as 'gateways' into discussing low performance areas.

The high performance 'gateway' is a way of dealing positively with poor performance issues by using an area of good performance as the 'way in' to discussing an area of poor performance. It is based on identifying and using discrepancies in someone's performance. For example, the salesman's relationships with customers are good, his relationships with colleagues are dreadful. Discussing the high performance area first provides a positive gateway into the problem. So the link could be expressed as follows: 'We've talked about how well you manage relationships with customers; do you put the same amount of effort into managing your relationship with the support engineers?'

## The salesman's agenda

If we look at the salesman's performance, there are likely to be several linked issues:

- He is far more effective at selling new business than optimizing existing accounts.
- He is good at account management and has excellent relationships with his customers.
- His time management and planning are weak.

This suggests that the issue is one of attitude rather than selling skills. It is likely that he prefers the buzz of selling new business to the less glamorous work of selling into existing accounts. The problem is to do with the priorities he sets himself and the way he manages his time to achieve them. By linking the issues in this way, two points become clear:

- There are several strengths to build on.
- Time management needs to be tackled early as a way of addressing the issue of his priorities (time management is usually another way of describing poor prioritizing).

Using his strengths as 'gateways' will help to construct a strategy for the discussion. For example, if you start by reviewing his success at selling new business, this can provide a positive entry to discussing why he is not so successful at selling add-on business.

This is likely to lead to the issue of time management and the need to shift priorities – the crux of the matter. Once this has been tackled, you can then move on to discussing his good customer relationships as the beginning of a discussion about improving his account management to ensure that he sells more to existing accounts. This will lead on to reviewing how he plans his activity so that you come up with a plan which ensures he meets your objectives while still using his ability to sell new business.

By linking issues in this way, you could end up with the following order for the agenda:

1. Selling new business.
2. Selling add-on business.
3. Time management.
4. Customer relationships.
5. Account management.
6. Planning.

This would be good in terms of climate too, although there is a risk in leaving planning so late, as this is where the specific actions will

Appraisal planner: stage 1

| Key job factor | Importance ranking | Effectiveness ranking | Reasons | Evidence |
|---|---|---|---|---|
| | 1 2 3 4 5 | 1 2 3 4 5 | | |
| | 1 2 3 4 5 | 1 2 3 4 5 | | |
| | 1 2 3 4 5 | 1 2 3 4 5 | | |
| | 1 2 3 4 5 | 1 2 3 4 5 | | |
| | 1 2 3 4 5 | 1 2 3 4 5 | | |
| | 1 2 3 4 5 | 1 2 3 4 5 | | |
| | 1 2 3 4 5 | 1 2 3 4 5 | | |
| | 1 2 3 4 5 | 1 2 3 4 5 | | |
| | 1 2 3 4 5 | 1 2 3 4 5 | | |
| | 1 2 3 4 5 | 1 2 3 4 5 | | |

**Figure 5.3** Appraisal planner: stage 1

be discussed. It is not so good in terms of momentum, because it is tackling the toughest problem area, his attitude, first, but that has to be tackled early to pave the way for agreement on the practical changes that need to happen.

Many managers allow the agenda for their appraisals to be driven by the documentation of their appraisal system, dealing with each issue as it is laid down on the form that they are using. This may be appropriate, but it is best to check this out, using the four factors: climate, momentum, priorities and linkage. It will not always be possible to satisfy all of them, as in the case with the salesman, but they will help you to plan a strategic route through the appraisal. Planning activity 5.4 gets you to plan a suitable agenda for your appraisee.

## PLANNING ACTIVITY 5.4: ORDERING THE AGENDA

There are three stages to this activity:

1. Use the map you have developed for the appraisal you have been planning through this chapter to create the most appropriate order for your agenda.

2. When you have done that, copy the finished agenda into the planning form (Figure 5.3), writing in the job factors in the order you have decided and their importance and effectiveness rankings. (If you do not want to write in the book, replicate the whole form on a new piece of paper.)

3. Fill in the two columns to the right of the rankings. These are:
   - **Reasons:** The reasons for your ranking of their effectiveness at each job factor. These can be entirely subjective.
   - **Evidence:** Any hard evidence you have or could collect to substantiate your reasons.

Figure 5.3, once completed, will give you a useful plan for your appraisal. It will help you to do the following:

- **Prepare** effectively by identifying hard data that you may need to gather beforehand.
- **Plan** how to tackle issues strategically and coherently.
- **Conduct** the interview in a structured and thorough way.

The planning form can also be used to help the appraisee prepare for the appraisal. This will be explored in detail in the last section in this chapter: creating the appropriate climate.

# Identifying outcomes

Having prepared your agenda for the appraisal interview, the next step is to identify what **outcome** you want to achieve from discussing each of the job factors. These outcomes will describe the change that you want to take place in each aspect of the person's performance to make sure that the specific goals are carried out successfully. They clarify the point you want to have reached by the end of the discussion, and so help you to manage it effectively. It is much harder to control an interaction if you are not clear about your desired outcome.

You will find it useful to have clear outcomes for each job factor, regardless of the effectiveness ranking. It is tempting, when you are preparing for an appraisal, to concentrate on the poor performance areas – in fact, all your planning time can get swallowed up by worrying about how to tackle the difficult issues. It is important to resist this temptation and to identify outcomes for areas of adequate and high performance as well as for underperformance.

In my experience, many of the problems that managers experience in their appraisals are caused by the identification of inappropriate outcomes. Sometimes this is because managers do not spend enough time rigorously clarifying what their outcomes are. Sometimes it is because they simply get it wrong (because it is hard to get right). Below are the three most common mistakes that I come across.

## Outcomes and solutions

Many managers cause themselves no end of trouble by not making the distinction between outcomes and solutions, not just in appraisals, but in any persuasive situation. In the area of performance management, the distinction between the two can be defined as follows:

- The **outcome** is the change that you want to happen to the person's performance.
- The **solution** is the way that this change is to be achieved.

For example, you may want somebody to improve their time management: this is your desired outcome. The way you decide to achieve this outcome is to send the person on a training programme: this is your solution.

The mistake that is often made is that, rather than focusing on the desired outcome, we 'lock into' a specific solution and try to persuade someone to agree to it, i.e. to go on the training programme rather than improving her time management. There are two things wrong with this:

1. There is probably more than one solution which could achieve the desired outcome – the one we have identified may not be the most appropriate or effective.

2. We are more likely to generate resistance to a specific solution than a desired outcome. And once the solution has been resisted, it is much harder to get agreement to the outcome.

Case study 5.1 gives some real-life examples of times when managers have suffered from confusing outcomes and solutions.

## CASE STUDY 5.1

A manager wanted some information from a senior manager. He arranged a meeting: it was cancelled. This happened three times. He became increasingly frustrated. He didn't consider other ways of getting the information, but became locked into the need to meet the senior manager. He did not need to meet him to get the information.

- Inappropriate outcome: meet the senior manager to get the information.
- Appropriate outcome: get the information from the senior manager.

A senior technician was given the task of improving the relationship between a group of engineers and the laboratory technicians on a factory site. He decided that the way to do this was to arrange fortnightly meetings. After two meetings, people stopped coming. The relationship between the two groups deteriorated as a result. The inappropriate solution defeated the desired outcome.

- Inappropriate outcome: get the two groups to meet together regularly.
- Appropriate outcome: get better collaboration between the engineers and technicians.

A senior manager wants to improve the ability one of her people to work in a team. She sends him on a groupworking skills programme. He resents this hugely, hates training, hates interpersonal skills training in particular, is shy, and awkward, does not want to be part of a team. He refuses to gain anything from the programme, goes back to work more stubbornly resistant than ever, and his relationship with his manager has deteriorated.

- Inappropriate outcome: get him to go on the groupworking skills programme.
- Appropriate outcome: get him to contribute more in team meetings.

In each of the three examples in the case study, there are several possible solutions that could be used to achieve the desired outcome.

## EXERCISE 5.3

Spend a few minutes now reflecting on examples from your own experience when you have caused yourself problems by locking into a specific solution rather than focusing on your desired outcome. If you cannot think of examples from your own experience, think about some of the people you work with.

Focusing on the desired outcome before thinking about solutions will help you to do the following:

- Clarify the change you want to see.
- Think of a range of possible solutions.
- Consider the other person's preferences.

## Ideas and action

I once observed a manager attempting to persuade an engineer during his appraisal that the safety procedures on the chemical plant where they worked were essential. He got nowhere. The engineer thought that *safety* was essential, indeed he had the best safety record on the site, but he thought that the procedures were an overelaborate waste of time and he had more important things to do than jump through hoops for the bureaucrats in head office. They argued about this for a long time.

The manager told me afterwards that this was not the first time he had had that conversation, almost word for word, and he never got anywhere. And the sad thing was that, although this was his best engineer, he could not recommend him for promotion because he did not follow the safety procedures. As a result, the engineer was becoming increasingly bitter and disillusioned and it was becoming harder to manage him.

The manager's problem was that, by choosing to persuade the engineer that the safety procedures were essential, he had made his desired outcome focus on *ideas* not action. He wanted the engineer to agree to the principle of safety procedures, and got nowhere (wasting a lot of time getting there). The outcome he actually wanted was for the engineer to follow the procedures, and he did not have to persuade him to *agree* with them to do that; it would be nice if he did, but it was not necessary. If the manager had focused his desired outcome on the **action** he wanted the engineer to take, he could then get him to weigh the advantages of taking that action (promotion) against the cost (hassle).

- Appropriate outcome: get him to use the safety procedures rigorously for the next month.

## EXERCISE 5.4

Spend a few minutes now reflecting on examples from your own experience when you have caused yourself problems by focusing your desired outcomes on ideas rather than action. If you cannot think of examples from your own experience, think about some of the people you work with.

If you anticipate the other person being resistant to the changes you want to see, you will almost always need to focus your desired outcome on actions rather than ideas. This will help you to:

- Avoid fruitless and repetitive arguments.
- Control the scope and focus of the discussion.
- Devise an effective strategy for persuading the other person.

### Steps and staircases

The third mistake is that managers identify outcomes which are too big to be achieved in one go – they go for the whole staircase rather than taking it one step at a time. I have often set outcomes for people that have been unrealistic because I have failed to understand and anticipate the difficulties they will have in learning something that has become second nature to me. It is better for me to break my outcomes down into the steps that need to be taken for that outcome to be achieved. This helps me to assess whether it would be better to have an outcome which will include some of the steps rather than all of them.

For example, I was once trying to help someone who had just joined a company I was working for, to evaluate his priorities more effectively. He was trying to do too much at once in order to impress people and was having the opposite effect. This was true in the way that he related to me: he wanted to learn everything at once and did not use his time with me effectively because he wanted to discuss too many issues.

Initially I set myself an outcome which was to get him to prioritize his use of time better. He agreed with the need to do so, but found it enormously difficult. He was too stimulated by his new working environment and too keen to prove himself. I realized that my outcome was unrealistic, a huge demand to make of him in the circumstances. I decided to set a more specific outcome: to get him to plan how best to use the review meetings with me in terms of prioritizing his learning.

This second outcome was far more achievable. It provided a useful first step towards the broader outcome and at the same time made our meetings more rewarding for both of us. He learnt, by thinking through his needs for each meeting, ways of prioritizing which he was able to apply in other areas of his work.

- **Appropriate outcome:** prioritize use of me as coach.

## EXERCISE 5.5

Spend a few minutes now reflecting on examples from your own experience when you have caused yourself problems by identifying desired outcomes which were overambitious. If you cannot think of examples from your own experience, think about some of the people you work with.

If you anticipate that the other person is going to have difficulty in achieving the changes you want to see, you will almost always need to focus your desired outcome on steps rather than staircases. This will help you to:

- Reduce any resistance to change.
- Develop achievable solutions.
- Avoid failure experiences.

Planning activity 5.5 gets you to identify suitable outcomes for the appraisal you have been planning in this chapter.

## PLANNING ACTIVITY 5.5: IDENTIFYING OUTCOMES

Identify your desired outcomes for the discussion of each agenda item from stage 1 of your appraisal planner, bearing in mind the points made above by focusing on:

- Outcomes rather than solutions.
- Actions rather than ideas.
- Steps rather than staircases.

When you have identified your outcomes, copy the key job factors from stage 1 of the planner on to the form (Figure 5.4): stage 2. Then write down your desired outcome for each job factor in the appropriate column. NB Do not fill in the solutions column at this stage. (If you do not want to write in the book, replicate the form on a separate piece of paper.)

It can sometimes be harder to identify meaningful outcomes for high performance areas than for job factors where there is an obvious need for improvement. There are three ways in which you can build on people's strengths, by setting outcomes which focus on:

- **Sustaining** their current level of performance, especially if their working conditions are likely to change or become more difficult in the coming period.
- **Improving** their already high level of competence so that they can achieve tougher targets and standards.
- **Optimizing** their strengths by using them in new areas, increasing their responsibilities or maximizing their contribution.

*Managing people*

Appraisal planner: stage 2

| Key job factor | Desired outcome | Possible solutions |
|---|---|---|
|  |  |  |
|  |  |  |
|  |  |  |
|  |  |  |
|  |  |  |
|  |  |  |
|  |  |  |
|  |  |  |
|  |  |  |
|  |  |  |

**Figure 5.4** Appraisal planner: stage 2

Managers often complain that they do not have the time to do as much planning for their appraisals as they would like. This may well be true but it is more likely that they do not use the time they do set aside very well. If all you did in your planning time was think long and hard about your desired outcomes, I guarantee that you would conduct more effective appraisals as a result.

# Diagnosing performance problems

So far you have identified the following:

- An overall objective which defines where you want each of your people to be by the end of the year.
- Specific goals for one of your people which define the activity that he or she will be carrying out during the year.
- Outcomes for each agenda item of his/her appraisal which define the performance change required if the specific goals are to be achieved.

You now need to identify the problems that are likely to stop people from achieving these various levels of objective. The third stage in the planning process is diagnosing the symptoms and causes of underperformance.

I shall provide you with a simple tool which will help you to think through in a structured way why people might not be doing something as well as you want them to, or why they may have difficulties in carrying out new tasks or responsibilities. It is based on four questions which, between them, cover all the likely causes of performance problems. They can also be used to anticipate the likely problems someone will experience with a new task or responsibility. They are as follows:

- Does he have the **knowledge** and experience to do the task well?
- Does she have the **skills** to apply her knowledge and experience?
- Does he have the right **attitude** to the job or task to allow him to apply his knowledge and experience skilfully (attitude includes confidence)?
- Are there **external blocks**, outside her control, which are causing her to underperform?

The answers to these four questions can be arranged to provide you with an easy-to-read 'map' which summarizes your diagnosis. Figure 5.5 illustrates this by showing a diagnosis of why the

| Knowledge | Skills |
|---|---|
| • Clarity about my priorities:<br>• Lack of experience of selling | • Not good at selling to non-technical people<br>• Needs to use more questions with senior managers rather than rely on expertise<br>• Not good at getting past the gatekeeper |
| • Investment in doing the 'big sale'<br>• Lack of confidence in unknown territory<br>• Likes being the expert | • Engineer is not helpful (but whose fault?)<br>• Tough targets tip him towards the big sale<br>• Big territory to cover |
| Attitude | External blocks |

**Figure 5.5** The diagnostic map

salesman from our earlier example may be underperforming in the
job factor of selling add-on business. In this figure, there are causes
of underperformance in all four quarters of the map. This will not
always be the case. Sometimes, the causes may be solely lack of
experience, for example; at other times, the issue may be a
combination of skills and attitude problems.

## *PLANNING ACTIVITY 5.6: THE DIAGNOSTIC MAP*

Select one of the job factors from your appraisal planner where you want
the person to improve their performance. Reflect on the causes of their
underperformance, using the four headings

| Knowledge | Skills |
|---|---|
|  |  |
| Attitude | External blocks |

structure your thinking.
   Replicate the diagnostic map on a separate piece of paper and use it to record
your thoughts.

The most common difficulty people have with the diagnostic map
in Planning activity 5.6 is making a clear distinction between
attitudes and skill. It can be hard to know for sure whether someone
actually lacks skill, or whether lack of confidence, for example, is
preventing its use. If you are in doubt, it is safer to put it down as
an attitude issue. Otherwise, I hope you have found the activity
straight-forward and useful.

The diagnostic map is a simple tool for clarifying your thinking
about someone's performance. In particular, it forces you to think
beyond your immediate assumptions about why a person is under-
performing. It also provides you with the basis for planning how to
help somebody to improve their performance. We will be looking at
this in the following section.

## Strategies and solutions

Once you have diagnosed the causes of underperformance, you can
start to think about the strategies and specific solutions that will be
required to help the person overcome these problems in order to
achieve your desired outcome. We will start by looking at two

different types of strategy to performance problems and then look at the range of solutions that exist within each type. They are:

- **Management strategies:** To create a change in the attitude of the person or in the working environment.

- **Development strategies:** To improve the person's capability to perform aspects of the job.

The diagnostic map can be used to identify which type of strategy is required and thus help you to decide as a manager on the most effective solution and on the nature and extent of your involvement. Figure 5.6 shows the type of strategy that is appropriate for different causes of underperformance. This simple distinction will help you to make some basic decisions about how best to help people improve their performance. If there are causes in only one quarter of the map, you will be able to see clearly what type of strategy is required. If, as is more common, there are causes in more than one quarter, the following guidelines will help you to decide which quarter to address first:

- If there are external blocks, you should first decide whether it is within your power to remove them, or at least reduce their impact. If so, your first steps should be management solutions to minimize the impact of the external blocks.
- If there are attitude issues, these need to be addressed before any attempt is made to provide development solutions. Attitude

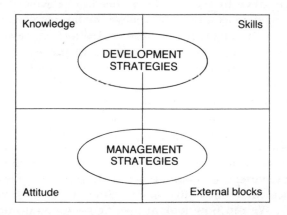

**Figure 5.6** Identifying the appropriate strategy

issues have to be managed: if they are not, it is unlikely that the required changes will happen. Developmental activity might take place at the same time, but should never be a subsititute.

● If there is a lack of knowledge or experience and a lack of skill, it will almost always be better to put the knowledge or experience in place first.

## EXERCISE 5.6

Spend a few minutes now reflecting on how you would tackle the salesman's underperformance at selling add-on business. Decide the sequence in which you would address the issues that are shown in the diagnostic map of the salesman (see page 97).

Your starting-point for Exercise 5.6 will depend on whether you feel you had room for manoeuvre over the external blocks. The size of the salesman's target and territory may be outside your control and, even if they are not, you may not want to change them anyway. The relationship with the engineer is a problem, but not sufficiently serious to suggest that it should be your starting-point.

It will probably be best to start by addressing the attitude issues. Before taking steps to develop the salesman's confidence, you will have to help him to recognize that being the expert is not enough when selling to non-technical people; you will also have to persuade him to let go of hunting the big sale so that he gets a few more small ones. He will have to accept that he needs to develop confidence and skills in new areas if he is to achieve the targets you are setting. There is no point in investing time and effort in developmental activity until he is committed to changing in the ways you want. When you have managed the attitude issues successfully, it will be time to consider your strategy for developing his skills and experience and the specific solutions you will use to do this.

## Solutions

We have explored how the diagnostic map can help you to decide what kind of strategy is required, which issues to address first and the sequence in which to tackle different causes of underperformance. We can now look at specific solutions in more detail. Figure 5.7 shows some of the options that exist under the broad

**Figure 5.7** Solutions

headings of management and development strategies as they apply to the different causes of underperformance.

You will probably be able to add options to this list that are more relevant to your particular working environment. When identifying which solutions are appropriate, you should bear the following points in mind:

- Development solutions should not be used to tackle management problems.
- Development strategies should involve as much on-the-job learning as possible. This is usually how people learn best, because they have the opportunity to apply their learning immediately in the setting for which it is intended.
- On-the-job development solutions involve creating learning opportunities and providing the coaching and support to ensure that the opportunities are used well.
- Off-the job training is almost always only a partial solution. If it is to be effective, it must be part of a broader development strategy which involves on-the-job learning.
- Development strategies and solutions should be discussed and agreed with the learners, so that they can influence and are committed to the outcome.

## EXERCISE 5.7

Spend a few minutes now reflecting on how you would tackle the salesman's underperformance at selling add-on business. Decide the specific options you would use to address the issues that are shown in the diagnostic map of the salesman (see page 97).

How you tackle the saleman's attitude issues will depend on the kind of person he is. It may be appropriate to confront the issues head on, meeting him to give him some direct feedback about your concerns with his attitude in order to persuade him to change his thinking. If you feel he will be resistant to this approach, it may be more effective to set tight targets which make it clear that his performance will be measured in part by the extent of the add-on business he sells.

In order to develop his capability to sell to non-technical decision-makers, you will need to first increase his exposure to that kind of selling situation, sending him out with more experienced sales people. Then you could help him to review these experiences in order to plan similar sales calls in his own accounts. You could accompany him on a number of these calls to support him and give him feedback before leaving him to do them on his own.

## PLANNING ACTIVITY 5.7: STRATEGIES AND SOLUTIONS

Identify your preferred solution for each of the job factors on your appraisal planner. This might be a series of steps, such as the coaching strategy just suggested in the comment to Exercise 5.7. When you have done that, put yourself in the other person's shoes and think of a solution the appraisee might prefer which would be acceptable to you. Then consider other options that might also be acceptable.

Write your options in the solutions column of stage 2 of the appraisal planner on page 96, or, if you do not want to write in the book, on the form that you have replicated.

You may find it difficult to think of more than one solution for some of the job factors when completing Planning activity 5.7. The reason you were asked to do so was to encourage you to:

● Consider the appraisee's response to your preferred solution.

- Avoid getting locked into one solution.
- Prepare acceptable options so that you can be more flexible during the appraisal interview.

Sometimes, however, there is only one solution that is acceptable to you, so if you struggled to find alternatives, do not worry. It is better to know that you only have one option because you have rejected the alternatives than because you have not considered them.

---

## Creating the appropriate climate

---

I have not met many managers who look forward to doing their appraisals. Even the ones who enjoy managing people tend to dislike them. There are three reasons for this, characteristics of the appraisal interview which have a negative impact on the 'climate' or atmosphere of the interaction. They are as follows:

- The appraisal interview starkly exposes the imbalance in **power** between appraiser and appraisee.
- Discussions in appraisals often get things out of **perspective**, by focusing on the negative aspects of the appraisee's performance.
- Appraisals are usually a **formal** interruption of the informal, daily relationship between a manager and their people.

To some extent, these problems are an inevitable feature of the appraisal. But it is possible to manage things, both before and during the interview, in order to minimize their impact. In this chapter, we will look at what you can do beforehand. We will also look at what you can do during the appraisal to manage the climate effectively in Chapter 7. Before we look at these issues in more detail, do Exercise 5.8 to raise your awareness of the impact of the climate on the effectiveness of appraisals.

### *EXERCISE 5.8*

Spend a few minutes now reflecting on times when you have been appraised. To what extent has the climate of the appraisal been affected by issues of power, perspective and formality as described above? How have these issues affected how you felt about being appraised?

## Power and control

By definition, managers do have more power than the people they manage. Most of the time this is not a problem: it is an accepted part of working life, and the imbalance is usually integrated into the daily reality. Come appraisal time, the imbalance is painfully apparent: she is going to decide my salary for next year; he can influence whether I get the promotion I am after; she could set me targets that make my life a misery; he is going to tell me whether the quality of my work is acceptable. The appraiser has all the power.

This is a fact of life, but it is an awkward one, because it makes the appraisal more difficult: the appraisee can feel suspicious, defensive or threatened as a result. It tends to make the manager feel uncomfortable and nervous. It is stressful. The interview would be a lot more productive if the stress of this imbalance was reduced. So the problem is how the power in an appraisal can be shared more equally between appraiser and appraisee.

The first answer is conceptual, but an important general point for managers. There is a difference between *power* and *control*. It is easy to confuse the two, or to see them as one and the same thing. We often hold on to the power in a situation because we want to retain control, but it is possible to **share power without losing control**. And the appraisal is an example of a time when it is absolutely desirable to do that. It is in both parties' interest for:

- Appraisees to feel that they have some power in the appraisal.
- The appraiser to retain control over the interview.

The second answer is eminently practical. It is not the only way that you can share power in an appraisal, but it is a good one, and illustrates clearly what is meant by the difference between power and control. It is a process for involving appraisees in planning and preparing their appraisals. The process has three steps:

1. Give a copy of a blank stage 1 of the appraisal planner (page 88) to the appraisee and ask him or her to list job factors and rank them in terms of importance and effectiveness. You could work from an agreed set of job factors, or ask the appraisee to generate them.

2. Meet before the appraisal interview (say two weeks before) to compare your planners. Identify differences and discuss their impact on the appraisal. Do not try to resolve any differences at this meeting.

3. Use this pre-meeting to agree:
   - An agenda for the appraisal.
   - Actions that need to be taken beforehand, e.g. evidence that could be collected, people who could be spoken to, etc.
   - How best to conduct the appraisal.

These three steps will help you in several ways:

- They will prevent any nasty surprises surfacing during the interview.
- They will clarify the nature and extent of any differences in opinion and so help you plan the appraisal more effectively.
- They give appraisees the chance to reflect on your perception of their jobs and performance and so help them prepare for the appraisal more effectively.
- They give you and the appraisee the chance to revisit issues and/or look for hard evidence to back up what each of you is saying.

Allowing appraisees to plan appraisals with you in this way gives them some power in the situation and so reduces the imbalance of power. It does not, however, undermine your control of appraisals. You are still in control of the process and will be in control of the interview itself. Use Exercise 5.9 to consider whether this process would be of value to you.

## EXERCISE 5.9

Spend a few minutes now reflecting on whether the process of sharing power through a pre-appraisal meeting as just described would benefit you with your appraisals. First consider the benefits. Then consider whether it would cause you any problems.

Most people who decide to use this process find that it helps them to prepare for appraisals more effectively, as well as having a positive impact on climate. The most common objections are as follows:

- **Time** – and I accept that if you are appraising a lot of people, this kind of process could be impractical, although it does generally cut down the length of time of the appraisal itself.

- **Control** – some managers feel that it is risky to give people the opportunity to obtain evidence to support their point of view. I think this is generally managers' way of saying that they do not feel comfortable sharing power.

# Keeping perspective

Just as there is a tendency when you are planning appraisals to concentrate on the areas of poor performance, so there is a tendency to allow the appraisal interview to be dominated by discussion of these same poor performance areas. This is not intentional; it is just that these areas often require longer discussion, especially if there are differences of opinion. But there are risks to getting sucked into the poor performance trap, such as:

- The problem areas get out of perspective: if you spend 80 percent of the time discussing poor performance, it will seem that you think 80 percent of the appraisee's performance is poor!
- The appraisee feels demotivated as a result: underrecognized for what he or she does well, and persecuted for personal failings.
- You sink a lot of time and energy into areas of performance which will be the most difficult in which to generate significant change.

So here are three things to bear in mind when you are planning your appraisals that will help you to keep perspective and avoid these pitfalls. Plan to:

1. Spend time exploring high performance areas. We tend not to address these areas with anything like the same rigour that we bring to bear on poor performance. Spending time *exploring* successes is much more motivating for appraisees than a few words of recognition. It may also help them to sustain their high performance, improve it or use their strengths in new and more rewarding arenas.
2. Make sure that you invest your time and energy focusing on areas of performance where improvement is possible and where the pay-off of such improvement will be significant. There will be some areas of poor performance where it will be better to accept that improvement is unlikely to happen than pretend that it is possible and spend a lot of time getting nowhere.

3. When discussing an issue, find a balance between focusing on analysis and solutions. The poor performance trap usually involves discussion about the nature, extent and causes of a problem. Although this is necessary, unless the analysis leads to discussion of how to move forward, the discussion will tend to be circular and unproductive.

If you follow these three steps, you will find it easier to keep perspective during the appraisal and create a positive, purposeful and productive climate. Use Exercise 5.10 to consider this further.

## EXERCISE 5.10

Spend a few minutes now reflecting on the last appraisal you conducted (or if you have not been an appraiser before, the last time you were an appraisee). Think about how you (or your appraiser) managed the appraisal in terms of the three points just made:

- Did you spend substantial time exploring high performance areas?
- Did you invest your time and effort wisely, or did you concentrate on areas where improvement was unlikely to happen?
- Did you strike a good balance between analysis and solutions?

## Formality and informality

You will probably already have an established relationship with your appraisees. You will have managed them for months, if not years. You may once have been their peer, promoted over them when the opportunity arose. Your relationship with each person will have its own characteristics and dynamics that are acted out and developed every day you spend together during your working lives. You will have established a way of behaving towards each other that underpins the effectiveness of your relationship at work.

The kind of relationship you have established in order to coexist in the normal working day, however, may not be appropriate during an appraisal interview. The appraisal is a highly formal interaction, with a precise function where each person's role is rigidly defined. If one or both of you attempt to bring your everyday relationship into the interview, it could cause problems, especially if you deny the formality of the occasion. In most cases, there is a need to establish a new way of relating just for the duration of the appraisal interview. People often recognize this need and instinctively adapt their behaviour, sometimes appropriately, sometimes not.

## Groundrules

As a relationship becomes established, it develops its own set of 'groundrules' which govern the way people behave towards each other. These groundrules develop automatically, usually without any discussion or conscious decision-making. Some of them will be positive, some less so. You may have a groundrule with one of your people, for example, that says: it's OK to make jokes about the incompetence of senior management, or it's OK to be cynical about the organization, or it's OK to make fun of each other, or it's not OK to be openly critical of each other, or it's not OK to give each other positive feedback. Groundrules such as these may not cause problems normally. But they could make an appraisal interview extremely difficult.

## *EXERCISE 5.11*

---

Spend a few minutes now reflecting on the groundrules that have been established in your everyday relationship with the person you have been using in the planning activities. Might any of these groundrules cause problems during the the appraisal interview?

---

If you find it difficult to do Exercise 5.11, compare your relationship with the appraisee with your relationship with someone else. Are there differences in terms of what it is OK to do and not OK to do? Are there things you could say to one person that you would not say to the other, for example? Exploring the differences in this way will help you to identify the groundrules that exist in each relationship.

One of the ways you can use groundrules to actively prepare for and manage the climate in an appraisal is to do the following:

- Review the existing groundrules in your relationship with the appraisee to identify any that might be inappropriate for the appraisal.
- Decide how to manage these groundrules so that they do not disrupt the interview.

- Identify new groundrules that would be useful for you to establish specifically for the appraisal.

The kind of groundrules you might want to establish will depend on the kind of climate you want to create. If, for example, you want to confront a number of attitude issues during the appraisal, you will want to create a tough, honest and challenging climate. To do this you might want a groundrule that says 'it's OK to give critical feedback', or 'try not to react defensively to criticism'.

Here are some examples of groundrules that managers have recognized that they will need to establish to create an appropriate climate for one of their appraisals:

- Do not assume that what I say is right.
- No negative comments about senior management.
- No excuses.
- No sidetracking – keep to the issue being discussed.
- No assumptions that you know best.
- Do not apologize for your lack of experience.
- No gossiping about other members of the team.
- No third-party feedback.
- Tell me if you are not committed to what we agree.

The establishment of these groundrules will not guarantee that people will behave accordingly. They are only a statement of intent. Their value is that they have raised potential problems and established principles for how they can be avoided or dealt with. These principles can be referred to if the problem does arise during the interview.

## Environmental issues

You also need to establish groundrules which manage the environment in which the interview takes place. These should cover issues such as:

- Location.
- Seating arrangements.
- Time.
- Interruptions.
- Note taking/form filling.

For example, it may be best for the appraisal to take place on neutral territory, away from your office (and particularly your telephone!). You may want to agree a finish time, or that the interview will go on as long as necessary. It might create a more appropriate climate if you did not sit with a desk between you. It may be better to fill in the appraisal documentation at the end of the interview, rather than having it on the table between you during your discussion. People have different preferences about these issues. It is important to discuss them with the appraisee so that you can agree together how you want the appraisal to be conducted. Use Exercise 5.12 to consider how such environmental issues apply to your appraisals.

## EXERCISE 5.12

---

Spend a few minutes now reflecting on:

- The environmental groundrules that you would like to establish with your manager at your next appraisal.
- The environmental groundrules that you established, directly or indirectly, the last time you appraised somebody.
- The environmental groundrules that you think the person you are focusing on in the planning activities would like at his or her next appraisal.

---

If you intend to meet with your appraisee before the appraisal, it might be appropriate to discuss groundrules then, agreeing together what kind of behavioural and environmental groundrules you would both like to have in place for the interview. If you are not having a pre-meeting, you could do this at the beginning of the appraisal itself. It is best to involve the appraisee in establishing groundrules. This is another way of sharing power – sharing responsibility with appraisees for managing the *process* of the discussion as well as the content. They are likely to have demands to make about the way they want you to behave towards them.

When you do Activity 5.8, you may feel that you do not need to take any steps in order to ensure that the climate for the appraisal is appropriate; or that if you did do something, it might inhibit the appraisee rather than help them to feel more relaxed. On the other hand, you may see one of the options above as a way of managing a difficult relationship or situation.

## PLANNING ACTIVITY 5.8: CREATING THE APPROPRIATE CLIMATE

First decide what kind of climate you need to create to achieve your desired outcomes for the appraisal you have been planning. For example, does it need to be critical, challenging, open, positive...? Then decide how best to create the appropriate climate for the appraisal you have been planning. This might involve one or all of the following:

- A pre-meeting to plan the appraisal with the appraisee.
- Management of the agenda so that you keep perspective.
- Establishing appropriate groundrules.

If, for example, you have been promoted above your peers and are having to appraise them for the first time, you will be confronted with the need to establish new groundrules: the peer relationship is no longer appropriate. If you work in a matrix management structure, you may be appraising people who are more experienced than you, even senior to you; or you may be appraising people who have been working under a project manager for most of the year and with whom you have had little direct contact. A pre-meeting to establish how best to manage the appraisals will be necessary.

# Summary

In this chapter we have focused on five stages in preparing for and planning an appraisal interview. These are as follows:

1. **Preparing the agenda** – what you want to discuss in the most effective order.
2. **Identifying outcomes** – the change that you want to see in a person's performance.
3. **Diagnosing performance problems** – identifying the causes of underperformance.
4. **Planning solutions** – the strategies and solutions for achieving your desired outcomes.
5. **Creating the appropriate climate** – the climate you need to establish in order to achieve your desired outcomes.

This planning process should help you to structure the time you give to planning appraisals so that you use it efficiently and productively. Many of the tools and messages contained in the five stages are not applicable only to appraisals; they apply more generally to the management of people. You will probably have already started linking them to other aspects of your job and relationships at work.

In the next chapter of Part 2, we shall be looking at ways of planning your coaching activity. Most of the stages in the appraisal planning process are of direct relevance here, particularly identifying outcomes, diagnosing performance problems and planning solutions. We will not repeat them in the next chapter; instead we will assume that you are planning your coaching activity having just completed your appraisals – and thus will have gone through these three stages for all of your people.

Before you move on to the next chapter, you may find it helpful to do Exercise 5.13 and Planning activity 5.9.

## EXERCISE 5.13

Spend a few minutes now reflecting on how you could apply what you have learnt from the appraisal planning process described in this chapter to other aspects of your people management and your work in general.

## PLANNING ACTIVITY 5.9: APPRAISAL PLAN 2

Plan the appraisal of another of the people you manage, going through all five stages of the planning process on a new subject. This will help you to consolidate your learning from this chapter. It will also give you another option when you do the coaching plan activites in the next chapter.

# 6

# Planning coaching

So far in Part 2, you have:

- Identified overall objectives, specific goals and management processes for each of your people.
- Planned how to appraise one, possibly two, of your people and so identified whether the improvement of their performance requires management or development solutions.

In both cases, you will have started the process of planning your coaching activity. You will have identified which people you should be working with to develop their performance and capabilities through the work on overall objectives. And, from planning their appraisals, you will possibly have identified aspects of their performance which require coaching solutions.

In this chapter we shall look in more detail at how to plan your coaching activity effectively – your activity at the micro-level of the performance management cycle illustrated in Figure 6.1.

Before we do, it is worth explaining what is meant here by coaching, which is **an attempt to help people to do their job better.** There are several definitions of coaching, and this one is not necessarily the most accurate. I use it because, when I talk to managers about coaching, I often feel that they perceive it as something alien to their experience – a kind of management activity that they do not do now and are unlikely to find the time to do in the future. In fact, managers are 'coaching' their people all the time – but they tend not to regard what they are doing as substantial or significant enough to be classified as coaching.

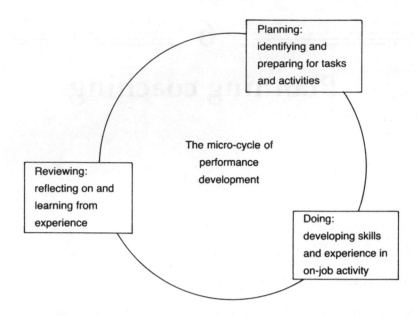

Planning: identifying and preparing for tasks and activities

The micro-cycle of performance development

Reviewing: reflecting on and learning from experience

Doing: developing skills and experience in on-job activity

**Figure 6.1**   The micro-cycle of performance management

What they are doing is *helping* people, in an on-going, low-level way, to do their jobs better – and there is little difference between the help that they are offering and what might be described as coaching activity. This help can take many forms. It ranges from a brief exchange in the corridor to planned involvement in the development of new skills over a long period of time. In this book, these are both regarded as coaching contributions, because they are both attempts to help someone to develop skills and performance. It is by reflecting on and valuing the many and various ways that you help people at the moment that you will be able to increase and improve your coaching contribution. Use Exercise 6.1 to do this now.

## *EXERCISE 6.1*

Spend a few minutes now reflecting on the various ways you help the people you manage to do their work better. Think back over the last week and identify five times when you offered some kind of help to someone. Nothing is too small – a word of advice or encouragement is enough to be included on your list.

There are very few managers that I have come across who do not do any coaching of their people. But in most cases, the coaching that they do is *reactive*: if someone comes to them with a problem, or needs help of some kind, they will give it to them; if they see someone doing something wrong or struggling with a piece of work, they will give advice and help to sort things out. There are fewer instances where managers coach *proactively*, making their contributions and interventions according to a plan which aims to achieve a targeted improvement in someone's performance.

# Being proactive

Although reactive coaching is valuable, it tends to have the following shortcomings:

- It focuses on the achievement of tasks rather than the improvement of performance.
- It is triggered by problems and difficulties and so can fail to reinforce good performance.
- It is *ad hoc*, and so does not provide a coherent learning and development process.

In this chapter, we shall look at how you can plan your coaching effort so that you are being **proactive** in helping your people improve their performance and develop their capabilities. Being proactive means having a clearly defined plan of action for how you are going to help them achieve a specific improvement in one or more aspects of their performance. The planning process that you will be going through will help you to **prioritize your coaching effort** so that you use the time that you can give over to coaching to best effect, and to **identify helping strategies** so that you offer people the kind of help that they will find most useful at the most appropriate time.

The activities in this chapter will enable you to draw up coaching plans for those of your people whom it is appropriate for you to be coaching. The first step will be to decide who these people are.

---

# Prioritizing your coaching effort

---

Most managers would agree that they do not do as much coaching as they would like to do, and the reason they give for this is lack of time. It is undoubtedly true that most of you will not have the time to do as much coaching as you would like to nor as much as is required. But it is worth reflecting on how well you use the time you do make available for coaching and whether you are investing that precious resource wisely, i.e. getting a good payback for your effort.

There are generally three mistakes that are made:

1.  Managers try to coach too many people at once, spreading themselves too thinly and so not spending enough quality time with anybody to achieve the desired results.
2.  Managers focus their effort on their poorest performers even when there is little realistic chance that these people will improve significantly.
3.  Usually as a result of (2), managers will neglect those people who can improve significantly with relatively little coaching input.

## *EXERCISE 6.2*

> Spend a few minutes now reflecting on whether you make any of the three mistakes just described in the coaching that you do.

The planning process you are about to embark on will help you to avoid these mistakes. If you are avoiding them already, it will give you a structure which may help you to recognize how you have avoided them and to keep on avoiding them in the future.

The first step of the planning process is to see yourself as a scarce resource that has to be deployed carefully and strategically if it is to be used well. This may mean the following:

*   Focusing your coaching on one or two people at a time.
*   Having a rationale for whom you coach when.
*   Prioritizing key performance areas for development.
*   Identifying clear targets within which to limit your contribution.

We will work through each of these in turn. When we have finished, you will have drawn up the first stage of your coaching plan.

## Who should you be coaching?

If you do not have a lot of time and you are managing a group of several people, you need to decide where best to focus your coaching effort if you are to coach proactively. To make this decision you need to assess your people against four factors. You will have used three of them when identifying your overall objectives earlier in Part 2. They are:

- **Competence:** Their ability to do their job to the standard that you require.

- **Potential:** Their potential to improve their performance and to develop their careers within the organization.

- **Motivation:** Their desire to improve and their readiness to learn and develop.

- **Pay-off:** The benefit to be gained if they do improve their performance.

Often managers respond only to the competence issue: if someone is not doing their job well enough, they will try and help them to do it better. But if the person does not have the potential to improve, or is not motivated to do so, you have to decide whether the effort that will be required to coach that person is justified by the pay-off that you are likely to achieve. If the answer is that it does not, coaching will not be the appropriate solution. Case study 6.1 offers two examples from a clinic that I once ran for a group of sales managers.

## CASE STUDY 6.1

Jack had been trying to help one of his salesmen, Bill, to improve his planning so that he used his time more strategically. But Bill did not have the potential to improve – he was in his 50s, an old sales dog who was not willing or able to learn new tricks! Jack had spent some time trying to coach him and had failed, getting increasingly frustrated in the process. In the end, he decided that, rather than try to improve Bill's planning skills, he was just going to make sure that his two-monthly plans were OK. So now he meets with Bill every eight weeks to draw up a two-monthly plan with him, with no expectation that any learning or skill development will take place.

Jill has been trying to improve the performance of her best salesman, Ron. He certainly has the potential to improve, in fact he could go a long way in the organization. However, he does not think he needs to improve, does not like being managed by a woman, and sees any attempt by Jill to coach him as an infringement of his freedom. In short, he does not have the motivation to improve. But, more importantly, given Ron's already high level of performance, any pay-off that Jill could achieve through coaching him will be far outweighed by the effort she would have to put in to overcoming the obstacles. Given that she was also managing two less experienced salespeople, she decided to focus her coaching effort on them and leave Ron alone until he became more comfortable with her as his manager.

We have seen how, at the macro-level, it is important to set yourself the right overall objective for your people and how managers often set objectives targeted at performance development when they should be targeted at activity management. This is an example of the same issue at the micro-level: Jack was initially making a very common mistake – coaching somebody whom he should just be managing.

In both examples, the managers have been drawn in to coaching somebody where the effort involved far outweighs the pay-off to be gained. This is because they have not used all four factors (competence, potential, motivation and pay-off) to assess the situation. Jack got drawn in by focusing on competence. Jill got drawn in by focusing on potential. Exercise 6.3 will help you to see whether you have made similar mistakes to those initially made in the case studies.

## EXERCISE 6.3

Spend a few minutes now reflecting on where you focus the coaching that you do. Use the four factors (capability, potential, motivation and pay-off) to assess whether you are investing your time in the right people.

To summarise the key messages:

- You should focus your coaching effort on people where the effort of improving performance is justified by the pay-off that that improvement will bring.

- To do that, you need to decide whether the effort will be too great, or whether the pay-off will be substantial.
- You must avoid sinking too much time and effort into people who are unlikely to respond positively to your coaching, either because of lack of potential or motivation.

By assessing your people against the four criteria, you will be able to identify where it is best to invest your time and effort. Some people are likely to have the potential and motivation to bring significant pay-off for relatively little effort. There may be others whom you feel are not worth coaching at all. This does not mean that you have to stop helping them: it means that you should not be *proactively* trying to develop their capabilities. The kind of help you offer is more likely to involve managing their activities with them rather than helping them to learn and develop.

## Who should you coach when?

### EXERCISE 6.4

Spend a few minutes now reflecting on this question: If you could only coach one of your people at a time, in what order would you coach them?

It is unlikely that you will ever have to focus on only one person at a time, and I am not suggesting that you do. Exercise 6.4 is useful in helping you sort out your priorities, and it will be important for you to do that if you manage a large group and run the risk of spreading yourself too thinly by trying to coach too many people at once.

In Case study 6.1, Jill was sorting out a sequence for her coaching activity which was based partly on the overall needs of her team and partly on the personalities of the people involved. It is likely that she will use her time better if she focuses on the two inexperienced salespeople now, leaving open the possibility of working on Ron's development later. There are several reasons for this:

- The two salespeople need her help more.
- She needs them to come up to speed as soon as possible so that she can cut back her own selling activity.
- Leaving Ron alone for a while will probably be better for her relationship with him.

- She needs to be less dependent on Ron's performance in case the relationship does not improve.
- Helping the other two will be more gratifying. They are highly motivated and will help Jill develop her confidence as a coach.

So strategically, Jill's decision to focus on the two new salespeople was a smart move. It matched her own and her group's overall needs in the medium term, and it is needs of this kind that should be shaping your coaching strategy. In order to identify them, you may have to do the following:

- Predict when high performers are likely to want to leave the group (e.g. in order to further their careers).
- Anticipate dips in the performance of your high and adequate performers.
- Evaluate the potential of low and adequate performers to develop their performance and become high performers.
- Assess the time that it is likely to take to develop low and adequate performers to the required level.
- Be realistic about the amount of time you can commit to developing people's performance.

These are not easy judgments. In other circumstances, for example, it may have been appropriate for Jill to focus on Ron for a while so that his performance compensated for the other two while they were learning the ropes. Or she may have decided to develop Ron's coaching skills so that she could delegate to him some of the work of developing the new salespeople. There are countless possible strategies, depending on the particular circumstances that you are in. The key point is to **think strategically** about the way you organize your coaching activity. Planning activity 6.1 helps you to do this.

## PLANNING ACTIVITY 6.1: COACHING STRATEGY

Start your coaching plan by identifying a strategy for your coaching activity which establishes:

- Which of the people you manage you are going to coach proactively (i.e. make a conscious and planned attempt to improve their performance and capabilities).

- If there is more than one, the order in which you are going to put them in terms of focusing your coaching effort (i.e. who are you going to start with, etc.).

Make a note of the decisions you have made, as they will need to be entered in to your coaching plan later in this section.

## What aspects of their performance should you develop?

When our coaching is reactive, we tend to focus on the worst aspects of a person's performance, the issues that most urgently need addressing, the areas that have most impact on the job. Unfortunately, these are also likely to be the hardest issues to address, where it will be most difficult to achieve significant improvement. This may be because it is an activity which people genuinely struggle to do well, or one where they are resistant to the idea that they need to improve. Either way, many coaching relationships founder because of a failure to make headway on a critical performance issue. Exercise 6.5 asks you to consider how you focus your coaching activity.

## *EXERCISE 6.5*

Spend a few minutes now reflecting on how you focus your coaching effort in terms of areas of performance. Do you tend to invest your time and effort on problem areas where significant development will be difficult to achieve?

Poor performance issues clearly need to be tackled at some time. The question is: when? And the answer is: if possible, not at the beginning. It will be better for both of you if you can start by focusing on issues where someone is already performing adequately, where improvement is unlikely to be too difficult to achieve, and where it is unlikely that there will be too much resistance. Figure 6.2 illustrates this, by showing the degree of effort, pay-off and risk involved in focusing on different levels of performance. Risk here refers to the risk of failing to achieve the desired improvement in performance.

Focusing initially on areas of adequate performance increases the

| Level of performance | Effort | Pay-off | Risk |
|---|---|---|---|
| Low | High | Medium | High |
| Adequate | Medium | High | Medium |
| High | Low | Low | Low |

**Figure 6.2** Prioritizing what to coach

chances of your coaching generating tangible improvements. This can be beneficial in three ways:

- It will develop a positive basis and momentum for the coaching relationship.
- It may develop greater self-confidence or self-awareness which will make it easier to tackle the more difficult issues.
- It may develop knowledge and skills which can be applied to other performance areas.

So when you are proactively planning your coaching activity, you need to:

- Identify *all* the aspects of people performance which you want to help them improve.
- Decide the best sequence for tackling the different aspects.
- Start with the aspects where significant improvement will be relatively easy to achieve.
- Avoid falling into the trap of tackling the most urgent issue first if there is a risk that you will fail to achieve your desired outcome.

## When do I stop coaching?

The final stage in the proactive planning process is to decide when you will stop coaching someone on an aspect of performance. Deciding this will enable you to:

- Work towards clear targets within time limits.
- Have clear break points when you can review progress and evaluate your effectiveness.
- Allocate your time appropriately amongst the people you are coaching.

## EXERCISE 6.6

Spend a few minutes now reflecting on whether you have clear targets in mind for your coaching activity which will help you to assess when you can stop coaching someone on a particular aspect of performance.

There are two kinds of target that you may have set yourself. These are **performance targets**, which specify the standard of performance you want people to achieve by the time you finish coaching them; and **time targets**, which specify when you will stop coaching people on aspects of their performance, regardless of the standards they have achieved by that time.

Performance targets can often be hard to specify, but will be helpful in clarifying exactly what you want to achieve through your coaching. The process of clarifying them forces you to think through what is achievable and this helps you to set more realistic expectations for yourself and to plan your coaching contribution accordingly. It will help if you can attach objective measures to these performance targets, but hard measures are not essential: there are many areas of performance (especially relationship and interpersonal issues) where an attempt to define objective measures is counterproductive. The key is for you to have a clear and specific idea about the change in performance you are trying to achieve.

Time targets are easier to set. They should be determined by the amount of time you feel is required to achieve the intended improvement in performance. This should be balanced by the need to focus on other aspects of performance or other people within the group. You should be ruthlessly honest with yourself about the amount of time you can realistically commit within the time period you have allocated.

## *PLANNING ACTIVITY 6.2: PRIORITIZING*

Fill in stage 1 of the coaching plan, Figure 6.3, by following these instructions (use a separate piece of paper if you prefer):

1. In the 'Who' column, write down the name of the first person you are going to focus on.
2. In the 'What' column, write down the one or more areas of performance that you are going to focus on, in the order in which you intend to address them.

3. In the 'Where to' column, write down the performance target you have set to indicate the standard you want to have helped the person achieve by the time you stop the coaching process.

4. In the 'When' column, write down the dates when you intend to start and stop coaching on each of the performance areas for that person.

5. Return to the 'Who' column, write down the name of the next person that you will focus on and repeat steps (2) to (4).

6. Repeat this process until you have covered all the people you intend to coach.

The main purpose of Planning activity 6.2 is to encourage you to think proactively about your contribution as a coach. You may feel that it provides you with a working tool that you can use through the year to co-ordinate your coaching. Or you may have found that it is too structured to help you manage the reality of your working life, and does not reflect the nature of the work that you do or the people that you manage. Either way, I hope that it has given you the opportunity to stand back and evaluate some of the decisions you have made instinctively about how you spend your coaching time.

Coaching planner: stage 1

| Who | What (aspect of performance) | Where to (indicator of desired change) | When | |
|---|---|---|---|---|
| | | | Start | Stop |
| | | | | |
| | | | | |
| | | | | |
| | | | | |
| | | | | |
| | | | | |
| | | | | |

**Figure 6.3** Coaching planner: stage 1

# Identifying helping strategies

Having prioritized where you should focus your proactive coaching effort, it is now time to explore what form your coaching should take. There are several options for helping someone to do something better. The knack of being an effective coach is to pick the right option to meet the needs of the individual and the situation. In this section, we shall look at identifying the appropriate strategies for helping people by focusing on the following:

- The factors that influence your choices.
- The timing of the help you offer.
- The nature of the help you offer.

## Influencing factors

First, we shall explore some concepts which affect the transfer of learning from one individual to another. We will later see how these concepts underpin two practical decisions you have to make about the way you organize your coaching contribution.

Two main factors influence your instinctive choices about how you help people. They are, on the one hand, the amount of **control** you want to retain in the situation; and, on the other, the amount of **freedom** the learner wants to be allowed. The resolution of the tension between these two factors is the key to the success of any learning relationship. As coach, your management of this tension is determined by your perceptions of the third factor: **risk**.

### Control

Control and freedom are clearly interlinked. The more control you want to have as coach, the less freedom the learner will have, and vice versa. This will manifest itself at every level in the coaching relationship. It will determine what you delegate and how you delegate it; the extent to which you encourage the learner to explore, to do things differently, to take risks; the way you react when someone asks for help.

For example, if someone comes to you with a problem, your instinctive response may be to immediately give them the answer to the problem, expecting them then to go away and implement your solution, coming back to you if they need any more help. In this scenario, you are keeping tight control over the transfer of learning:

learners have little freedom to reflect on why they are having difficulty, to examine the processes by which you came to your solution or to explore other options which may be applicable.

## EXERCISE 6.7

' Spend a few minutes now reflecting on how you respond instinctively when people come to you to ask for your help with a problem. Do you tend to tell them how to solve the problem? Or do you help them to work out a solution for themselves?

A lot of the managers who come on my programmes perceive coaching as a process of giving people the right (i.e. the manager's) answer. They do not consciously see themselves as retaining control at the expense of the learner's freedom when they do this. They are conforming to the dominant learning model that they grew up with and which is still prevalent: the teacher is the repository of all knowledge; the learner absorbs the knowledge of the teacher. In this model, coaching becomes teaching, and the coach, like the teacher, retains control at the expense of the learner's freedom.

There is no doubt that this model has its advantages: it is quick, straightforward, relatively low risk and task oriented. And some-times it will be absolutely appropriate – but only sometimes. For the deficit of this model is that it does not involve learners in thinking things through for themselves, and therefore cannot ensure that significant learning has taken place. Learners may be able to complete the tasks satisfactorily, but will not necessarily be able to overcome the same or a similar problem the next time it presents itself. They may have to come back to you to ask for the same or another solution.

Your need for control will show itself most clearly in the way you delegate tasks and responsibilities. If your need is very high, you will probably not delegate much at all; when you do, it is likely that your briefing will be very detailed, you will tell people how you want them to do the task, and you will monitor their progress very closely. If your need for control is low, you are likely to delegate more frequently, and once you have outlined what the task is, let people sort out their own ways of doing it.

### Freedom

As learners, we all have different needs for freedom depending on who we are, what we are learning and the circumstances in which we are learning it. There are times when I am happy to give over control completely to the coach (when I learnt abseiling I wanted to be told exactly what to do!), and there are times when I want to be given the freedom to find things out for myself. I want to take risks, explore things in my own way, learn from my mistakes, come up with my way of doing things (even if it is the same as everyone else's – at least I will have discovered it for myself). Sometimes I want to manage my own learning and sometimes I want someone to manage it for me.

This choice is determined by my perception of risk: there are some risks which, although challenging, are acceptable to me; there are others, like abseiling, which are not.

For example, when I first started selling training, I wanted to be given the freedom to get out there and start doing it – and to learn from my experience. I wanted to develop my own style, to explore how I could use my personality to establish relationships with customers. If the person coaching me had tried to retain too much control and thus denied me the freedom I wanted, I would have reacted negatively, resisting his teaching, becoming impatient and over-anxious to prove my competence. To his great credit, he did not. He trusted me enough to let me loose, and provided enough support to ensure that I did learn from my experience and did not make too many mistakes. Use Exercise 6.8 to consider how this applies to you as a learner.

## EXERCISE 6.8

Spend a few minutes now reflecting on your own need for freedom when you are in a learning situation and how that need varies depending on circumstances.

There are times when learners want the freedom to take more control over their own learning, which means that, as coach, you may have to let go of some of your control. What you have to decide, in each coaching situation with each person, is whether it is appropriate to do so – whether it is in the learners' best interests to be given the freedom that they want. And this is where risk comes in.

### Risk

In each situation, coach and learner will have their own perceptions of the risks involved and their own subjective responses to those risks. For example, my manager knew better than I did the cost of my blowing a sale. But his own experience and maturity meant that he kept this risk in perspective – something I only fully appreciated when I was myself in the position of developing people's selling skills. It was then also that I fully appreciated the extent to which my perception of the risks involved were subjective, and could be entirely different from someone else's.

As coach, it is your responsibility to decide how much control you need to retain and so how much freedom to give the learner. In order to make good decisions, you need to assess the risks involved as *objectively* as possible, so that they are not based entirely on your subjective perceptions. You need to assess the following aspects of risk:

- **The task:** Can you afford to let the learner fail? For example, there were some prospects which were too big for my coach to let me manage on my own – the costs of failure were too great. But there were some situations where, although failure was undesirable, the consequences were not disastrous and were outweighed by the potential gain in terms of my learning and development.

- **The learner:** Can the learner afford to fail? For example, particularly in the early stages of my development as a seller of training, my confidence was fragile; too much failure too early might have led me to believe that I could never make it. If my coach had said from the beginning, 'get out there, kid, you're on your own!', he would have been giving me an inappropriate amount of freedom in the early stages of my development.

- **The coach:** Can you afford the learner to fail? There may be situations where the learner's failure will make you vulnerable. For example, my manager's reputation rested in part on his success in setting up a new division of the company. If he gave me too much freedom and I failed to deliver the goods, his reputation could suffer far more than mine.

## EXERCISE 6.9

Spend a few minutes now reflecting on an instance when the way you have helped somebody to learn has been influenced by your perception of the risks involved? Did this perception lead you to take more or less control over the learning process? Alternatively, think of an instance when somebody has been helping you to learn or develop a skill.

Because most managers coach reactively, it is likely that their instinctive response is one where they keep control – because they are working from their *subjective* assessment of risk (see Exercise 6.9). It is only when you are more proactive about your coaching that you will give yourself the time to evaluate the risks *objectively* in order to decide how much freedom to give the learner. There are two questions you can ask yourself that will help you with this evaluation.

**How likely is it that the learner will fail?** Because risk is involved, our judgment is often clouded by an instinctive focus on the downsides: the difficulty of the task, the consequences of failure. Under the weight of these concerns, we can underestimate our learners' competence and assume that they will fail. It is better to start by assessing learners' ability to carry out the task or activity successfully before thinking about how likely they are to fail.

**What would the consequences actually be if they did fail?** Just as we often underestimate learners' competence, we also tend to overestimate the consequences of things going wrong. Because of our emotional response to risk, we can end up making assumptions about what is at stake. It will help you to keep the size of the risk in perspective if you spend a few moments rationally thinking through what the consequences would actually be. They are often not as great as we imagine.

## EXERCISE 6.10

Spend a few minutes now reflecting on the risks involved in the situation you identified in Exercise 6.9. Was your assessment of the risks subjective? If so, use the two questions given above to check out your assessment and to review the appropriateness of how you managed the situation.

The assessment of risk is fundamental to the learning process. We have looked at it so far from the managers' perspective, in terms of how it influences their need to retain control. Learners also make an assessment of the risks involved in the situation, and this will influence their need to be allowed freedom. Having established the concepts, we will now go on to look at how these two assessments of risk can be managed through practical decisions about how to coach.

## Before, during and after

Coaching usually involves helping someone to do something well. The something may be an activity – selling business, using a computer, writing a report – in which the end results are tangible. Or it may be less well defined: communicating more clearly, thinking more strategically or managing time more effectively. In either case, coaching involves *doing*, and because of this, the coach has three possible points when she or he can intervene: before the learner does the activity, during the activity, and after the activity.

### Before

You will become involved before the activity in order to ensure that the learner prepares for it effectively, thus minimizing the risk of failure. The kinds of contribution you might make are as follows:

- Planning the activity with the learner.
- Reviewing the learner's plan.
- Helping to anticipate potential problems.
- Rehearsing key phases of the activity.
- Modelling how you would do the activity.

### During

You will become involved during the activity in order to see at first hand how the learner is doing and provide immediate feedback and support as well as a safety-net if required. The kinds of contribution you might make are:

- Observing without intervention.
- Providing on-going feedback.
- Joint conduct of the activity.
- Intervening in case of emergency.
- Modelling how you would do the activity.

### After

You will become involved after the activity in order to ensure that the learner has reflected on his or her experience during the activity and consolidated the learning from that experience. The kinds of contribution you might make are as follows:

- Giving feedback.

- Reviewing the activity with the learner.
- Replaying key parts of the activity.
- Summarizing key learning points.
- Clarifying how learning can be applied to future activity.

## EXERCISE 6.11

Spend a few minutes now reflecting on the extent to which you offer help to the people you are coaching before, during and after an activity. If possible, give rough percentages to the amount of your coaching time you spend in each category (e.g. before – 10 percent, during – 70 percent, after – 20 percent).

In reality, coaching does not always fall neatly into the three activities that you used in Exercise 6.11. The boundaries between them are blurred – you can help someone plan, do and review an activity within the space of the same interaction. This is particularly true if your coaching is reactive, when you are likely to be responding to problems identified during the activity; your intervention might be a combination of before, during and after contributions.

When you are coaching proactively, you can consciously decide when the most appropriate point to intervene will be: it might be at one of the stages, two or all three of them. The extent and timing of your involvement will depend on the decisions you have made about control and freedom. The more control you want, the greater the extent of your involvement, as Figure 6.4 illustrates.

Involvement at all three stages indicates a desire to minimize the

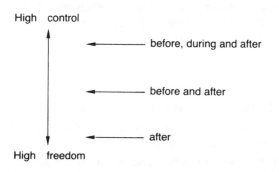

**Figure 6.4** Intervention and the control–freedom continuum

risk of failure by exerting control over the way the learner conducts the activity. You will reduce the amount of control and allow the learner more freedom as you feel that the risks associated with failure are reduced. For example, you may feel that it is enough to help plan and review the activity but not need to be there as they do it. As learners become more competent and self-confident, it is likely that the only contribution you will need to make is to review the activity to check on progress and to ensure that they are managing their learning effectively. And then the glorious day will come when you do not even have to do that!

## EXERCISE 6.12

Spend a few minutes now reflecting on an instance when you have been helping somebody to do something. Did you get the timing of your involvement right? Did you get involved too late, giving the learner more freedom than he or she was ready for? Did you get involved too early, taking more control than was appropriate?

Exercise 6.12 will probably have highlighted that the timing of your involvement has a major bearing on your success as a coach. This was brought home to me when I was coaching someone to write effective sales proposals. At first, I adopted a 'before and after' approach: we would talk about the proposal in outline; he would go away and write it; he would bring it to me and I would tear it to shreds! This proved not to be a useful learning process. There was one occasion when I so demoralized my colleague that I ended up rewriting the proposal myself (it was at this point that I realized things had to change). My mistake had been to overestimate my learner's need for freedom. For the next few proposals, we worked together during the writing period as well as before and after it. We broke the process down into a steps: objectives, structure, detailed plan, first draft and final draft. I helped him at each stage to make sure that he had it right before moving on to the next one. This made sure that:

- My colleague learnt the key stages of constructing a proposal.
- I could identify where he was having most difficulty.
- He had success experiences which provided good models for him and boosted his confidence.
- The final draft would only need minor alterations.
- We ended up with a good proposal.

Problems with the timing of our involvement often occur because we see an activity as having a single stage. Our familiarity with it blinds us to the complexity that will confront anyone who does not share our familiarity. By looking at the activity through the learner's eyes, and breaking it down into its key stages or components, you will be better able to decide the most useful points of involvement.

## Directing, guiding and enabling

The second practical consideration that will reflect the choices you have made about control and freedom is the way in which you offer help: your coaching style. We looked earlier at how the conventional model for transferring learning is one in which the control stays with the teacher. The essence of this model is that the teacher knows what is right and the learner does not, nor will the learner be able to find out unless told by the teacher. It works best when the purpose is to transfer knowledge and understanding. It works less well when the purpose is to develop skills: applying knowledge and understanding effectively. When that is the objective, the learning needs to be transferred in the way that best helps the learner to apply what has been learnt.

There is no one way of helping people learn that will work in every interaction. There are too many variables: the personality and needs of the learner, the complexity of the task and the time available. To be effective as a coach, you need to be able to use a range of coaching styles, and to select the style which best suits the requirements of the situation. We will now look at three coaching styles: directing, guiding and enabling.

### Directing

The directing style is closest to the conventional teaching model and, for most people, it is their most natural coaching style. Its main characteristic is that it involves the coach in **telling** learners things: what they did right, what they did wrong, what they should have done, what they should do next time, why they should do it like this, why they should not do it like that. The role for learners is to listen and learn and then do, according to the coach's vision of how things **should** be done.

Put like that, it is easy to be negative about the directing style, because the focus of attention is so much more on the coach than the learner. But I know from my own experience that the directing style can be appropriate. I was coached in the skills of how to write learning materials when I worked at the Open University by someone who used a high directing style – usually in the form of red ink lacerating my early drafts! – and I loved it, learnt from it and apply it to this day. Her style matched my needs and the amount of time we had to get it right. No problems.

## Guiding

The guiding style is characterized by a balance of telling and **asking**. The focus of attention is shared more equally between coach and learner because the coach is more interested in what the learner has to say. She may tell the learner the same things she would tell him if she was using a directing style, but she is also asking him things: Why he thought it went wrong? Whether he has had any ideas about how to do it better? Which of the various options does he think will work best? Why? What about if this happened though? And so on. The learner's role is to engage with the coach to explore each other's visions of how things **could** be done before agreeing together on the most appropriate option.

## Enabling

The enabling style is characterized by the high level of asking and the low level of telling. The focus of attention is almost entirely on the learner because the coach is mainly interested in what the learner has to say. She leaves her own opinions behind, concentrating on helping the learner to think things through for himself, asking questions to facilitate a process of exploration and discovery. These will be similar to the questions she would ask if she was using a guiding style, but there will be more of them, they will be more penetrating, and *there will be very little telling*. The learner's role is to respond to the stimuli being provided by the coach in order to reflect critically on his experience and identify his own vision of how he wants things to be done.

## EXERCISE 6.13

Spend a few minutes now reflecting on the coaching style you tend to use most often and the reasons for this. If possible, give rough percentages for the amount of your coaching that is done using each style (e.g. directing – 70 percent, etc.).

If your coaching is mainly reactive, the style you will use will probably be directing. This is partly because telling, for most people,

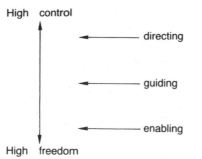

**Figure 6.5** Coaching style and control–freedom continuum

is their instinctive response if someone comes to them for help or if they see someone struggling with an activity. It is also because, when you coach reactively, you rarely have the time to use any other than a directing style, either because your own work has been interrupted, or because the learner wants an instant solution. Guiding and enabling take more time, and are more difficult, than directing.

When you are coaching proactively, you have to decide what style the learner will find most useful, not just in terms of the accomplishment of the activity but also in terms of the effectiveness of learning. The style you select will depend on the decisions you have made about control and freedom. The more control you want, the more a directing style will be appropriate, as Figure 6.5 illustrates.

As with the stages of involvement, your decision about style will be influenced by your perception of risk. If you cannot afford the learner to fail, and you think there is a risk of this, then you will use a directing style. If you feel the risk is low, you will feel better able to give the learner the freedom to explore things and are more likely to use an enabling style to ensure that the learner makes the most of the experience.

### Learning styles

We all have our preferred way of helping people to learn. Exercise 6.13 will have helped you to think about your own preferred style. For most people, this will be directing, for the reasons stated earlier: it is the style we are most used to; it is easier than the other two; it takes less time; it is task oriented. There are people who prefer guiding and enabling and who use these styles effectively. And there are some people who are able to use all three styles equally well, selecting the appropriate style depending on circumstances. It is these people who tend to be the most effective coaches.

Just as we have our own preferred coaching style, we also have our preferred learning style, and so do the people we are coaching. Some people like to be directed, some prefer to be guided, others only respond positively to being enabled. And this will vary depending on the circumstances. I wanted my coach to use a directing style when I learnt to abseil; I was happy to be directed by my coach at the Open University; I wanted to be guided and enabled when I was learning to sell training. Exercise 6.14 asks you to explore your preferred learning style.

## *EXERCISE 6.14*

Spend a few minutes now reflecting on your preferred learning style. Focus on the last time somebody helped you to learn something (not necessarily at work). What style was used? Did you get the kind of help you wanted? If not, what coaching style would you have preferred?

### Matching styles

Effective coaching occurs when there is a match between the helping style the coach is using and the style the learner wants them to use: the coach uses a directing style when the learner wants to be directed, and so on. If there is a mismatch, there will be problems. If the coach is using an enabling style and the learner wants directing, for example, then the learner is likely to feel confused, unsupported and inadequate. The other way round, the coach directing a learner who wants enabling, and the learner could feel frustrated, unrespected and undermined. Use Exercise 6.15 to consider how this applies with your own coaching activity.

## *EXERCISE 6.15*

Spend a few minutes now reflecting on times recently when you have tried to help someone learn something. Did your coaching style match the learner's preferred learning style? If it did, did you achieve the match deliberately or by accident? If it did not, did the mismatch cause any problems?

One of the coach's responsibilities is to try to ensure that she uses a helping style that matches the needs of the learner. The difficulty is in finding out what that style is. It would be nice if you could just ask the learner 'what kind of helping style would you like?' – but most people do not know – they are not used to thinking about how they learn best. Some people will be able to give you an answer and will be aware enough of their own needs to give you an answer that is accurate. But there are others who will tell you how they would like to be helped, or how they think they should want to be helped, and be quite misleading. The most common example is the person who asks for straight feedback and then becomes extremely defensive the moment you give it to them!

Getting the style-match right is usually a process of trial and error which is made easier if you have an awareness of the style you are using and a sensitivity to the way learners are responding. You can, however, try to anticipate their preferred learning style by thinking through how learners might perceive the risks involved. This is likely to be different from your perceptions, and will be based on two things: their sense of **competence** and their feelings of **confidence**. Learners will have a sense of the gap between their level of competence now and the level required to perform an activity. The bigger the gap, in their minds, the bigger the risk of failure. Learners will also have their own feelings of confidence in dealing with risk. Some will welcome the challenge, others will find it inhibiting. The level of confidence will determine the perceived size of the risk.

Just as your perception of the size of the risk involved will influence your need for control and so your coaching style, so learners' perceptions of risk and their confidence in dealing with it will influence the kind of help they will want from you. I have made mistakes as a coach in the past because I have over-estimated a learner's sense of competence: the activity seemed easy to me (I had forgotten how difficult I found it when I was learning). And I have also been insensitive to people's level of confidence, assuming that they would find the risks as stimulating as I would. It helps if you try to see things through learners' eyes and assess how they view their competence to do the activity sucessfully and their confidence to meet the challenge successfully.

## PLANNING ACTIVITY 6.3: HELPING

Fill in stage 2 of the coaching plan, Figure 6.6, by following these instructions (use a separate piece of paper if you prefer):

1. Transfer what you have written in the 'Who' and 'What' columns in stage 1 of the coaching planner into the same columns in stage 2.

2. In the 'Timing' columns, write down your decision about when to help against each entry in the 'What' column. Be specific wherever possible: for example, if you are going to help someone before the activity, write down in the 'Before' column what form this help will take.

3. In the 'Styles' columns, tick which helping style you intend to use against each entry in the 'What' column.

When you have finished Planning activity 6.3, you will have completed your coaching plan. Hopefully this will have helped you to think through and make decisions about how best to manage your contribution as a coach. Stage 1 of the plan should not change too much through the year. Stage 2 is likely to be more flexible. You should regard it as your opening shot, for the following two reasons:

● Your people's needs of you as a coach should change as the year progresses.

● You will make mistakes! It is hard to anticipate the learner's needs in terms of when and how to offer help.

Coaching planner: stage 2

| Who | What (aspect of performance) | Time of involvement | | | Coaching style | | |
|---|---|---|---|---|---|---|---|
| | | Before | During | After | Directing | Guiding | Enabling |
| | | | | | | | |
| | | | | | | | |
| | | | | | | | |
| | | | | | | | |
| | | | | | | | |
| | | | | | | | |
| | | | | | | | |

**Figure 6.6**  Coaching planner: stage 2

# Summary

In this chapter we have focused on two stages in planning your coaching activity:

- **Prioritizing your effort:** Deciding who to coach; when to coach them; what aspects of their performance to focus on; and what targets to set yourself.

- **Identifying helping strategies:** Deciding the timing of your involvement (before, during, after); and the nature of your involvement (directing, guiding, enabling).

This is the end of Part 2, which has focused on helping you plan your activity as a people manager. The intention has been to give you structures with which you can organize your thinking about the people you manage and make proactive decisions about how you are going to manage them. You may want to use some of the tools and structures after you have finished reading the book. The diagnostic map, for example, is a tool that many managers use as a quick way of clarifying their thinking before talking to someone about an aspect of their performance.

In Part 3, we shall be looking at the skills required to put your planning into practice: the interactive skills to conduct appraisals and coach people effectively. Before we move on to Part 3, Exercise 6.15 will help you reflect on the key learning points for you from Part 2.

## EXERCISE 6.16

> Spend a few minutes now reflecting on Part 2 of the book.
>
> - Identify five key learning points – things that you have thought about or realized when you were reading Part 2 that you feel will be helpful in improving your performance as a people manager. Write these down in the space provided overleaf.
> - Now identify one way that you can apply each of your key learning points at work. These should be specific actions that you are committed to carrying out.

| Key learning points | Actions |
| --- | --- |
| 1. | |
| 2. | |
| 3. | |
| 4. | |
| 5. | |

# Part 3

# Skills

Part 3 will help you to improve the way you interact with your people. It focuses on the behavioural skills required to manage formal and informal discussions about performance effectively. The exercises and activities in Part 3 give you the opportunity to reflect on how you manage interactions at the moment and to identify how to further develop your skills.

# 7

# Preface

## Interactive skills

Before you start reading Part 3, use Exercise 7.1 to think about your interactive skills.

*EXERCISE 7.1*

Spend a few minutes now reflecting on your effectiveness at communicating with people. Use the space below to note down what you think your strengths and weaknesses are:

Strengths                                    Weaknesses

There has been much discussion and exploration about why some people are better at communicating than others and there are many ways of addressing this issue. I shall focus on the behavioural aspects of communication – what people say and how they say it. There are other aspects which are equally important – the kind of person you are, your attitude to other people, body language. I am concentrating on verbal behaviour because that is the field I have been working in extensively for the last six years, and because I believe that it can provide you with clear structures for assessing your effectiveness and with practical steps for developing your skills.

In behavioural terms, effective communicators share the following attributes:

- **Self-awareness:** They tend to be aware of what they are doing as they are doing it. For example, they are aware of the degree to which they interrupt other people.

- **A range of options:** They have a wide range of options for how to behave. For example, in coaching terms, they will be able to use a directing, guiding or enabling style.

- **Flexibility:** They have the flexibility to adapt their behaviour according to circumstances. They can assess the situation, select the right option and behave accordingly.

In Part 3, we will be focusing on the first two of these attributes. By reflecting on the way that you tend to interact with people, you will develop greater self-awareness. This will be limited, however, by the accuracy of your self-perception – we all have more or less distorted pictures of how we behave. We need feedback from others if we are to develop a more rounded picture, and some of the activities will be asking you to obtain that feedback.

The main function of Part 3 will be to present you with ways of effectively managing certain types of interaction. Some of these will be part of your existing range of options. Others may be new, alternative approaches which you can build into your repertoire. Many of the activities will be asking you to consider whether applying these options will be appropriate for you given your situation at work.

What Part 3 cannot do is help you to become more flexible. This will only happen if you **practise** using those options that you think will be of benefit. There are lots of people who *know* how to communicate effectively yet who do not seem able actually to *do* it! The last skills activity in each chapter will give you a structure for applying what you have learnt.

# The five components

The skills we shall be looking at are those that are particularly relevant to managing appraisal and coaching discussions effectively. They will be explored in the context of those two specific types of interaction. Having said that, they are skills that can be applied to any one-to-one interaction and are also relevant to many group interactions, so although the focus is narrow, the application is broad.

The skills have been grouped under five headings. These five headings are, in my opinion, the five components of an appraisal interview that the appraiser needs to manage effectively. In fact, they apply to almost any interaction. They are as follows:

- **Climate:** Creating and maintaining the 'climate' or atmosphere that is most appropriate for achieving your objectives.

- **Clarity:** Providing clarity during the discussion in terms of its structure and also a shared understanding of issues, reactions and outcomes.

- **Content:** Managing the content of the discussion to ensure that each of you contributes in the way that will help you achieve your objectives.

- **Commitment:** Gaining commitment through the way you persuade people and develop solutions with them.

- **Confrontation:** Tackling and resolving difficult issues constructively, without causing unnecessary or damaging conflict.

## EXERCISE 7.2

Spend a few minutes now reflecting on the strengths and weaknesses you identified in Exercise 7.1. Do any of them relate to the five components described above? For example:

- Is one of your strengths that you make sure that you understand what the other person means?
- Is one of your weaknesses that you tend to avoid confrontation?

# Developing interactive skills

Each of the five components has its own specific requirements in terms of interactive skills, although there are general themes and principles that apply with all of them. The chapters build on each other incrementally, and the skills become more complex and sophisticated as you work through Part 3. We will be looking at interactions through a microscope, and there may be times when you find the level of detail unsettling: when interactions are dissected in this way, they can become unrecognizable from the conversations you have quite naturally at work. There are three general principles that will help you to make good use of this part of the book: choices, feedback and practice.

## Choices

We make choices about how we interact all the time. They are usually unconscious, instinctive responses to people and situations, but what you may regard as your natural interactive style is in fact a set of sophisticated choices that you have learnt as you have grown and developed. Most of them will have become second nature to you by now, so that your level of awareness of them is low. And this means that you tend to be unaware of the alternatives that exist. Because our choices are so entrenched, we believe that they are the only way to behave. As interactions are put under the microscope in the coming chapters, we will be exposing and dissecting the kind of choices you make all the time – it is just that they are not visible to the naked eye!

## Feedback

The exercises that you will be offered in Part 3 will sometimes ask you to reflect on the choices you make instinctively in order to heighten your awareness of them. It is only then that you will be able to evaluate their effectiveness and take more control over them. The trouble is that they are often so entrenched that reflection alone will not be enough. There will be times when it is suggested that you obtain feedback from other people about how they perceive your behaviour.

Asking people for feedback is potentially risky. To minimize that risk, here are some guidelines for you to refer to if you decide to get feedback about your interactive skills:

- Ask people who you can trust to give you **honest** feedback. These will be people who want to help you and who are prepared to challenge you if necessary.
- Explain why you are asking for feedback and what precisely you want feedback on. You should not be getting feedback about the kind of person you are, but on specific aspects of your behaviour.
- Hear the feedback people give you as *their* perception of you. This is not the 'truth' – it is just their perception, and says as much about them as it does about you. Try not to react defensively – you do not have to take it on board.
- Give yourself time to reflect on the feedback: do not reject it or agree with it too quickly. Think about it for a while to see if it is of any value to you before deciding what you want to do with it.

## Practice

Some of the activities in Part 3 suggest ways that you could practise the skills being explored. Practise is vital if skill development is to take place, but you may feel that the activities suggested are not appropriate for you. Here are some guidelines to help you identify alternative activities:

- Pick specific meetings or discussions in which you are going to practise doing something. You will only really practise a skill if you make a conscious decision to do it at a specific time.
- Pick low-risk practice opportunities, so that you can focus on your skill development without worrying too much about the outcome of the meeting or discussion.
- Set yourself achievable goals, so that you do not consciously try to practise too much at once. Focus on one or two skills or behaviours at a time – any more and you are likely to overload yourself.

# 8

# Climate

So far in this book, we have looked at climate in connection with preparing for an appraisal interview. Climate is a particular issue with appraisals because of the formal nature of the interaction. People's attitude to the appraisal process, their feelings about being appraised, their feelings about you appraising them, their feelings about you generally, all have a big effect on the climate that exists during the discussion. So do your feelings about them, their performance, appraisals, being an appraiser. Between you, you can generate a climate which could range from being cynical, suspicious, defensive and combative to open, constructive, challenging and supportive. The climate you generate will have a big influence on the outcomes you achieve and the commitment you each feel to them.

## EXERCISE 8.1

Spend a few minutes now reflecting on the kind of climate that existed when you were last appraised. Note down a list of key words that describe this climate (e.g. honest, constructive, critical . . .). Did you feel this climate was appropriate? If not, describe the kind of climate that you would have preferred by writing down another list of key words?

The key words in your second list in Exercise 8.1 may provide you with a set of generic climate 'indicators' that you could apply to all the appraisals you have to conduct this year. It is likely, however, that each appraisal will need to be different, to take the following into account:

- The personality of the appraisee.
- Your relationship with the appraisee.
- Your desired outcomes for the appraisal.

Although it is easier to talk about climate in the context of the appraisal interview, this will be true for *all* your interactions. They all have their own climate, shaped by the relationships, the expectations, the feelings about the issues and the way people behave. In this chapter, we will look at how you can generate the climate which will help you to achieve your desired outcomes for the interaction.

So far, we have looked at three ways of managing the climate *before* an interaction. These have been to:

- Share power before an appraisal by involving the appraisee in creating the **agenda** with you beforehand.
- Use **groundrules** as a tool to specify the kind of climate you would like to create for an appraisal.
- Choose a helping **style** which matches the needs of the person you are helping.

These steps can go a long way to creating an appropriate climate. But they have to be consistent with your behaviour *during* the interaction. I once watched the personnel director of a major computer company carefully establishing a groundrule about the appraisal being a two-way dialogue as a preface to talking at the appraisee for the next twenty minutes, using a heavy, and critical, directing style!

So now we are going to look at climate in terms of what you do during the interaction. We shall focus on three things:

- Starting up.
- Basic choices.
- Encouraging openness.

# Starting up

When interactions go wrong, the causes can often be traced back to things that did or did not happen in the first few minutes. This is because we tend to leap straight into the *content* of the discussion. It is not natural for us to hold back and spend a few minutes thinking about *how* to discuss the content – we just want to get on in there and discuss it. Some time later, you realize that this is not quite what the other person wants to discuss, or that things are getting pretty confused, you are not sure where all this is leading, or that the person is being very defensive even though he or she came and asked for your advice in the first place. Effective communicators tend to be very careful about the way they start an interaction so that a framework is established which focuses the discussion appropriately.

Use Exercise 8.2 to think about how you tend to start interactions.

## EXERCISE 8.2

Spend a few minutes now reflecting on how careful you are at starting interactions. Think about the last three times you had a performance-related discussion with one of your people. Did you dive straight into the content, or did you spend a few minutes first establishing how to manage the interaction? If so, what did you do in those few minutes?

The impulse to focus on content rather than process at the beginning of an interaction is hard to resist, and identifying and agreeing an appropriate process is not an easy thing to do. So we shall now look at the kind of issues you might need to discuss at the beginning of any interaction to provide you with a structure for establishing the process. To illustrate these issues, I shall use an impromptu coaching scenario as a case study to show that care needs to be taken even in what seem to be the most straightforward interactions, as well as the bigger set pieces.

## CASE STUDY 8.1

I am working at my desk, I am busy, harassed, the phone keeps ringing, the world is not allowing me to do what I want to do. Carrie pokes her head round my door:

'I'm sorry to interrupt, have you got a minute?'
I look up wearily, see the anxiety on her face, think, 'Is this how I make my people feel, anxious?', nod and try a smile.
'Come in', I say, 'what is it?'
'I need some advice about how to handle Max.'
I tell her what I think she should do, give her three options actually, off the top of my head, smile encouragingly and give out signals which say 'Can I get on with *my* work now, please?'
'Thanks', says Carrie, but she looks confused and anxious and she leaves the room slowly in the hope that I might notice.

I hope *you* have had interactions like this too! It took me some time to learn that when people ask for advice, it is not necessarily my version of advice that they need. There are three process issues that I did not establish with Carrie before I dived in to give her what I assumed she wanted. They are the same issues summarized earlier with regard to preparing for bigger interactions: agenda, ground-rules and styles.

## The agenda

I did not clarify what Carrie actually wanted to talk about. I interpreted advice as 'please give me three options', and I made that the only agenda item for our 'meeting'. In fact, options were the last thing Carrie wanted! Here are some other possible agenda items:

- Discuss the events that have led up to the problem.
- Analyze the causes of the problem.
- Review what Carrie has done so far.
- Consider the ideas Carrie has had for sorting it out.
- Evaluate the options for dealing with it.
- Help Carrie to come up with her own solution.

I should have checked out my assumptions by asking Carrie what she meant by advice. We should then have agreed what ought to be discussed in order to give her the help that she wanted, which might have included one or more of the above. In effect, although an agenda might seem overformal, we needed to agree a structure for the conversation.

## Groundrules

There were a number of unwritten groundrules that provided the basis for the short interaction with Carrie. They were:

- It is not OK for you to sit down.
- The interaction must be as quick as possible.
- I will not *really* stop what I am doing.
- You should be apologetic.
- I decide what you want.

The central message being: 'Carrie, you are inconvenient!'

I should have been clearer about whether I was going to offer Carrie significant time or not. I made the assumption that she needed the advice immediately, and this may or may not have been the case. If she did not, I could have asked her to come back when I had finished the letter I was writing. If she did, I needed to shift the groundrules so that the climate was more conducive to a helpful discussion.

## Styles

The scenario in Case study 8.1 is a good example of the difficulty of matching your helping style to the learner's preferred learning style, as discussed in Chapter 6. It sounds like Carrie wants a bit of directing – after all, she *is* asking for advice! And directing may be appropriate: if there is a crisis, the best thing in the short term may be to give her a solution to the problem. What I actually did was use a clumsy guiding style, giving her three options to evaluate and leaving the decision to her. This was the last thing she wanted – it did not help her think things through nor did it save her from having to do so!

The truth is I cannot know what kind of help Carrie wants or needs when she asks for advice. Advice is like help: it is a blanket word that means different things to different people at different times. I needed to find out what Carrie meant by it then, and the only way I could do that is to have asked her. Does she want me to tell her what to do? Does she want me to help her think it through for herself? Does she want to consider options or does she want a quick solution? I might not have agreed with her answers to these questions, in which case I could check it out a bit further, or even disagree with her. But in the end, we needed to come to an agreement about how I was to be of help.

All this might sound mighty complicated for a ten-minute chat. The trouble with talking about process is that it tends to sound more complicated than it is in practice. Case study 8.2 shows how the interaction with Carrie could have gone. In this second scenario, Carrie is more likely to feel less rushed and anxious, more relaxed and assured. She will feel that I have recognized her needs and am committed to finding the best way of helping her. She will feel reassured that the discussion has some shape and direction and that our roles are clear. She will feel confident that she will have decided on a course of action by the end. And she will feel that I regard her as important enough to take her concerns and her development seriously. If she does feel all those things, the benefit of spending a few minutes focusing on process will have been considerable.

## CASE STUDY 8.2

I am working at my desk, I am busy, harassed, the phone keeps ringing, the world is not allowing me to do what I want to do. Carrie pokes her head round my door:

'I'm sorry to interrupt, have you got a minute?'
'Is it urgent?'
'It is really.'
'OK. Come in. Sit down.'
I get up and pull my chair round to the front of my desk to show that she has my undivided attention.
'What's the problem?'
'I need some advice about how to handle Max.'
'OK. When you say advice, can you be a bit more specific about what kind of help you want? Do you want me to tell you what to do, or help you come up with your own decision?'
'I'd like to give you the background and then I want you to tell me what to do.'
'Have you thought of options yourself?'
'Yes, but I'm not sure what's best.'
'Why don't we review your options then, before I suggest anything?'
'OK.'
'What shall I do: just listen for a while, or do you want me to give you feedback or ask questions as you go along?'
'If you could just listen for a bit and then if you've got any feedback, I'd like to hear it.'
'OK, off you go then.'

Starting the discussion by agreeing the agenda, groundrules and style is likely to increase the effectiveness of all your people-management interactions. It may involve considerable self-discipline on your part to stop yourself from going straight to the content, but the rewards will be worth it. The process can be boiled down to one question: 'how can I best help you?' If you get into the habit of asking that question, it will stop you from diving into the content and from moving too quickly into solutions.

## *SKILLS ACTIVITY 8.1: STARTING UP*

Identify one interaction in the recent past which would have gone better if you had taken more care in the way you managed the process at the beginning: setting the agenda, establishing appropriate groundrules, matching styles.

Write a script for how the interaction could have gone if you had managed the process more carefully (in the way I rewrote the script of my interaction with Carrie.) Try to make the other person's responses realistic. You can 'write' the script in your head by imagining how the conversation might have gone. Putting it on paper will make it easier for you to evaluate it and modify it.

If you are not used to focusing on the process of an interaction, an exercise like Skills activity 8.1 can seem strange, awkward and artificial. It is a bit like riding a bike for the first time – you wobble around and look silly! The people you manage might also find it odd if they are not used to being asked how they want to be helped. If it does feel awkward to you, do not feel constrained by the kind of language I use (I am a consultant after all!). It is the principles that are important and you must use *your* language to express them rather than mine, and find ways of talking about how best to help your people which you feel comfortable with and which they can understand, accept and engage with.

## **Basic choices**

In Part 2, we looked at three ways of helping someone: directing, guiding and enabling. The main characteristic that was used to define these styles was the balance of **telling** and **asking** behaviours.

For example, the enabling style is characterized by high asking and low telling. This balance is a simple way of describing the basic choice that we have to make when we are talking to somebody. How much do I tell? How much do I ask?

Usually we make this choice unconsciously. It will be determined partly by our reaction to the specific situation, but partly also by our habitual behaviour. As we grow older, we develop patterns of behaviour which form our instinctive responses to situations and people. At the root of these patterns is the ask/tell balance. Most people, for example, tend to do more telling than asking: the exact balance will vary according to circumstances, but the pattern is fairly constant. Some people do a lot of telling and hardly any asking at all, whatever the demands of the specific interaction. And there are others who ask a lot of questions and do relatively little telling in most situations.

## EXERCISE 8.3

---

Spend a few minutes now reflecting on how you would describe yourself. Are you someone who generally:

- Does a lot of telling and not much asking?
- Does mainly telling with some asking?
- Asks a lot of questions?

---

Exercise 8.3 can be difficult to answer accurately: very few of us are aware of how much time we spend telling – although it is almost always much more than we think. This is because, when we are telling, our mind is taken up with what we are saying and what we are going to say. This focus on content makes us less aware of how we are behaving and how our behaviour is affecting other people. When we ask questions, on the other hand, we tend to be more aware of our behaviour because asking a question is more difficult: you are not just thinking about what you are saying, you are thinking about what you want the other person to say and how best to get them to say it. We tend to know when we have asked a question because we have been conscious of putting the words together. When we are telling, the words can tumble out automatically. Use Skills activity 8.2 to find out what you do.

## SKILLS ACTIVITY 8.2: TELLING AND ASKING

To help you get a more accurate picture of the balance of your telling and asking, here are two small activities:

- Listen to yourself: choose an interaction where your contribution is not vital and monitor your instinctive behaviour. See how many times your instinctive response was to tell; keep a check of how many times you asked questions.
- Get feedback: ask someone who knows you well and whom you trust to give you feedback about your behaviour generally. Do they think you do a lot of telling or not?

(NB Read the guidelines on asking for feedback on page 147 before doing this activity.)

Being aware of the amount of telling you do is one of the first steps towards becoming an effective communicator. In the training programmes I have run over the last six years, at least half of the participants have been people who do a lot of telling and relatively little questioning. Their effectiveness at work has been improved by learning when and how to ask more questions, because there are many situations when high telling/low asking style will be neither appropriate nor effective. And this is especially true in interactions that concern the management of people, because the balance of telling to asking has a major impact on climate.

The personnel director referred to earlier who established a groundrule about two-way communication before embarking on a one-way monologue is not untypical. It is much easier to know that you should ask questions than to actually ask them! In his case, the one-way monologue generated a negative climate, where the appraisee felt powerless, dominated, excluded and alienated. Although the impact will not always be so extreme, there will be few situations where it will be appropriate for an appraiser to have a high telling/low asking ratio. It is more likely to be useful in coaching situations where the learners need information and instruction and so need the coach to use a directing style to help them learn.

A high asking/low telling ratio is more likely to generate a positive climate in appraisals. By asking questions, you can show appraisees that you:

- Are interested in what they have got to say.

- Understand their point of view.
- Respect their ideas and opinions.

You are more likely to gain their involvement and commitment as a result. You are also more likely to gain the information you need to make fair assessments and constructive decisions. This is true for informal interactions as well: questions tend to have a positive impact on climate. You should only use a high telling style if you have made a conscious decision that it will best meet the requirements of the situation. Skills activity 8.3 will help you to apply this.

## SKILLS ACTIVITY 8.3: ASKING QUESTIONS

Identify one interaction in the recent past which would have gone better if you had done less telling and more asking. Note down the questions you could have asked that would have created a more positive climate and led to a better outcome.

At this stage in Part 3, I just want to establish the value of asking questions when managing people. If you are a habitually high 'teller', and want to do less 'telling', your first step should be to ask more questions. This will automatically reduce your telling, especially if you listen to the answers (which is not quite as obvious as it sounds). In later chapters, we will look at questions in more detail, exploring how different types of question can be used to help people understand and learn from their experience.

## Encouraging openness

Asking questions will encourage involvement, but it will not in itself encourage people to be open with you about their thoughts and feelings. And openness is often what is needed if the interaction is to be successful. You want appraisees to open up about how they feel about the job, their performance, their future, you. You want learners to be open about the difficulties they are having, their concerns, their failures and their successes.

Getting some people to open up can be very difficult. There are a number of reasons why they may not want to: they may be naturally quiet and shy; they may lack confidence that what they say will be of any value; they may be anxious about appearing inadequate; they may be suspicious about what you are going to do with the information. In most cases, their reluctance is because they do not feel that it is *safe* to be open.

The work that we have done so far in this chapter will help you to create an open climate. I am now going to focus on two ways that you can behave which will encourage people to overcome their reluctance by sending signals that it is safe for them to do so. These are: being responsive and modelling openness.

## Being responsive

One of the factors that will affect how open people are with you is the way that you respond to what they are saying. Your responses are a form of instant feedback which enables other people to assess whether what they have said is appropriate. Your responses can encourage them to say more and direct them towards a more appropriate contribution.

In people-management interactions, there are two things that tend to go wrong, although usually for the best of reasons: one is that we do not respond enough – often because we think that if we commit ourselves one way or the other we will 'close down' the other person. In fact, we are more likely to close them down if we deny them feedback, as this can create uncertainty and inhibit openness. The other is that we only respond positively – often because we want to create a positive climate. Unfortunately, if the responses we give are almost always positive, this raises doubts in the other person's mind about the value, or even sincerity, of our positivity. It can seem more like a strategy than a genuine response. This too can create uncertainty and inhibit openness.

## EXERCISE 8.4

Spend a few minutes now reflecting on whether your manager or supervisor does not respond enough, or responds mainly positively during discussions about your performance. Reflect on the impact that his/her responding behaviour has on you.

If you find Exercise 8.4 difficult, this may be because your manager is good at giving you clear responses to what you are saying, in which case you will probably not be that aware of his or her behaviour. It is more likely to have impact if his or her responding is too low. The impact then can be dramatic. When we do not get feedback in this way, we often imagine that the other person is disagreeing with what we are saying, although this is not necessarily the case. We can react to this perceived disagreement by becoming flustered and defensive. Use Exercise 8.5 to assess the way you tend to respond to people when you are coaching them.

## EXERCISE 8.5

Spend a few minutes now reflecting on times when you have been discussing performance issues with one of your people – they do not have to be appraisals. Consider whether:

- You have failed to respond enough to what the other person is saying.
- You have used positive feedback as a device to try to create a positive climate.
- You have suppressed your disagreement or negative feedback in order to maintain a positive climate.

As with our telling behaviour, our level of awareness of the ways in which we respond tends to be low – our responding behaviour is deeply habitual and entrenched. Some people respond very little, either positively or negatively. Others will disagree freely, but will tend not to express their agreement or support. Others will be the reverse, keen to be supportive but rarely disagreeing. The first step in improving your responding behaviour is to raise your level of awareness about the way you respond naturally and how that affects other people. Skills activity 8.4 will help you to gauge the impact of your responding behaviour.

## SKILLS ACTIVITY 8.4: RESPONDING

In order to get a more accurate picture of how you tend to respond, you will need to get feedback from the people you manage. Create an appropriate opportunity where you can ask them each individually whether they feel:

- You give them enough feedback.
- They are clear about what you think about them and what they say.

- You give them enough positive feedback.
- Your positive feedback is genuine.
- You disagree with them enough.
- You disagree or criticize them too much.

(NB Read the guidelines on asking for feedback on page 147 before doing this activity.)

There are three key messages to bear in mind. They are as follows:

- Make sure you respond to what the other person is saying. If you agree with it, verbalize your agreement; if you disagree with it express your disagreement. Do not leave what you are thinking unsaid – the other person will probably be imagining that you disagree.

- Do not go overboard with positive feedback and responses. They will not necessarily create a positive climate and you run the risk of devaluing later positive behaviour. Only give positive feedback and respond positively when these responses are genuine.

- Do not be afraid to disagree! People often make the mistake of assuming that disagreement will have a negative affect on the climate of an interaction. This is not the case. If the disagreement is rational and well considered, it is more likely to be perceived as a fair and useful contribution. Disagreement is only perceived as negative if there is a lot of it and there is not much positive feedback to balance it out. If you express your disagreement, your positive feedback will have far more value to the other person.

## Modelling openness

Responding clearly is one way that you can encourage someone to be open. The other way is to show that you are prepared to be open yourself: to 'model' how open you want the other person to be. To do this, we must first clarify what we mean by openness, which is a deceptively simple word!

It is best to see openness as having a number of levels: with some people you might share very little of your thoughts or feelings at all; with others you might share almost everything, your darkest fears, your wildest fantasies, your most secret secrets, your feelings about them, your feelings about yourself. These are two ends of a

## EXERCISE 8.6

Spend a few minutes now reflecting on different relationships in your life, both in and out of work. Think about how open you are in each of those relationships and about the different levels of openness that you choose. Are you as open with your boss as you are with your peers, for example? Are you more open with some of your peers than others? Think too about how you have come to choose the level of openness for each of these relationships.

continuum, and there are many levels in between. These different levels are like steps on a ladder. With most relationships, you start at the bottom of the ladder. Your choice about whether or not to take the next step is based on whether you feel it is safe to do so. And this will depend mainly on whether you feel the other person is prepared to take that step too.

The development of most close relationships involves a careful progress up the openness continuum, one step at a time, both of you together, in tandem. Problems in relationships often occur when, as illustrated in Figure 8.1, one of you goes faster up the ladder than the other. You are more open than the other person feels is appropriate, or you demand a level of openness in return

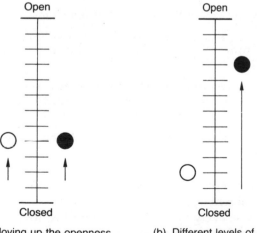

(a) Moving up the openness continuum in tandem creates a safe climate

(b) Different levels of openness will create tension in the relationship

**Figure 8.1**   The openness continuum

that the other is not ready to commit to. This generates uncertainty, anxiety, embarrassment. Exercise 8.7 helps you to relate this model to your own experience.

## EXERCISE 8.7

> Spend a few minutes now reflecting on instances when problems have been caused in a relationship by the distance between you and someone else on the openness continuum.

In most appraisals, the appraiser is, in effect, wanting the appraisees to zoom up the openness continuum on their own: to make themselves vulnerable in a way that the manager does not intend to do. Given that the appraisal is an interaction where the balance of power lies so clearly with the appraiser, it is not surprising that most appraisees decline the offer! If you want appraisees to be more open, you have to show them that it is safe for them to do so. The only way you can do that is to move up the ladder yourself, slowly and carefully. And given that you are the one with the power, you need to make the first move.

You can do this by sharing with the other person your own inner thoughts and feelings. Compare the following pairs of sentences:

- 'You had a really good year, last year.'
  'I'm really pleased with your performance last year.'
- 'You coped with the extra workload extremely well.'
  'I was impressed with the way you coped with the extra workload.'
- 'Your safety record in the lab wasn't that good.'
  'I was disappointed with your safety record in the lab.'
- 'Feel free to say what you want to me.'
  'I feel uncomfortable when you don't say very much in the appraisal.'

Although these pairs of sentences are saying the same thing, they will have a different impact on the receiver. In each case, the second sentence is more likely to encourage openness, for two reasons: you are talking about yourself as well as the other person – most of the sentences start with 'I'. You are using words that describe how you feel – 'pleased, impressed, disappointed, uncomfortable'.

By doing this, you are showing your willingness to be open and to take the next step up the openness continuum. You are signalling this clearly and so 'modelling' the kind of openness you would like from the other person. They may still feel that they do not want to respond in kind, but it is more likely that they will feel safe to do so. Skills activity 8.5 asks you to reflect on this.

## SKILLS ACTIVITY 8.5: MODELLING OPENNESS

Identify a recent discussion you have had about someone's performance.

- First, try to remember the extent to which you told the other person how you felt about his or her performance (as opposed to what you thought of it).

- Second, think of things you could have said in the discussion which would have modelled openness.

Refer to the earlier examples to help you with both stages of this activity.

Some people find it easier than others to describe their feelings. If you are not used to doing so, it can seem very artificial. But describing your feelings is a useful behaviour to have in your repertoire, so if you felt uncomfortable doing the activity – tell someone how uncomfortable you felt quickly! – it is worth persevering with it. Although modelling openness is particularly relevant to appraisals, where there are several inhibiting factors, sharing your inner thoughts and feelings will be useful in most interactions where it will help if the person is more open. We will look later at the use of this kind of behaviour when confronting difficult issues.

## Summary: managing climate

In this chapter we have looked at three aspects of actively managing the climate of an interaction.

### Starting up

Discuss and agree the 'process' for the interaction. This will involve some or all of the following:

- An agenda which provides the basic structure.

- The groundrules which underpin the interaction.
- The style in which you are going to help the other person.

## Basic choices

Control the amount of telling you do according to the helping style you have agreed.

## Encouraging openness

Encourage the other person to be open with you by:

- Giving genuine responses to what they say throughout the interaction, balancing negative and positive feedback as appropriate.
- Modelling in your own behaviour the amount and level of openness you want.

End this chapter by doing Skills activity 8.6.

## *SKILLS ACTIVITY 8.6: CLIMATE*

Identify a suitable opportunity for you to practise the lessons from this chapter. This will ideally be an informal discussion with one of your people about an aspect of their performance. Before you meet plan how you are going to create the climate you need to achieve your objective for the meeting. Decide:

- How you are going to agree a process for the discussion.
- Whether you should be mainly telling or asking, and if so what kind of questions you need to ask.
- How you can model the kind of openness you want from the other person.
- How you can ensure that you respond sufficiently and appropriately to the other person.

# 9

# Clarity

One of the reasons why appraisals are difficult is that they go on for so long – much longer than the interactions you usually have with the appraisee. Because of their length, it is hard to sustain a high level of clarity throughout the interview. You can lose structure as issues come up that you had not anticipated; you can lose direction if the appraisee diverts the discussion away from where you want it to go; the other person can say things that you are not sure you really understand; you can be unclear yourself – not spelling out the messages you want to send in ways that ensure that they are received. These problems are common in appraisals. They are not that uncommon with other, shorter interactions too! Sometimes this will not matter much – but it often does when the issues are about people and performance. In such discussions, the need for clarity is usually paramount.

In this chapter, we shall look at ways in which you can manage a discussion to ensure that there is as much clarity as possible. We shall focus on three aspects of providing clarity. These are:

- Structuring.
- Seeking clarification.
- Reacting clearly.

Although we are concentrating on a one-to-one interaction about people-management issues, the lessons contained in this chapter will have a general application to all kinds of interaction that you have at work, about any issue.

# Structuring

In Chapter 8, I said that when interactions go wrong, the causes can usually be traced back to the first few minutes. This is because of our instinctive preference for diving into the content of the discussion rather than establishing a process for how to best *manage* the content. One result of this is that the interaction lacks **structure**, and lack of structure tends to lead directly to lack of clarity.

One way of managing the process is to establish the 'agenda', because it is this which provides the structure, laying down what is to be talked about and in what sequence. Establishing the agenda at the beginning, however, will not guarantee that it is kept to during the interaction. It needs to be actively managed throughout the discussion if clarity is to be maintained. This is called structuring: providing the interaction with clear shape and direction. Case study 9.1 is an example of structuring behaviour, that explains what is going to happen in the rest of this section.

## CASE STUDY 9.1

We shall start by looking at the two kinds of behaviour that you need to use to establish and manage structure. Then we shall look in more detail at how to establish an appropriate structure in interactions where difficult issues are being discussed. At the end, there will be an activity which will help you to practise these skills. First, here is an exercise which asks you to think about the extent to which you structure your interactions at the moment.

## EXERCISE 9.1

Spend a few minutes now reflecting on two or three substantial interactions that you have had with people in the last week. Did you spend time at the beginning establishing a structure for these interactions? If you did, how did you do it? If you didn't, do you think the interaction lacked clarity as a result?

## Giving directions

It will help if you think of an interaction as a road journey. Your destination is your desired outcome (helpful also to realize that, if you are not clear about your desired outcome you are more likely to get lost!). Then you can think of the structure as your route. This will probably be made up of a number of sections: home to motorway; M6–M61; M61–M62; M62–M1; M1–office, for example. Each section is different, but leads in sequence to the next and on towards the final destination. Each section requires different approaches from you, the driver: home to motorway through a complicated one-way system in light traffic; M62 stuck in traffic jam for long periods and so on.

Establishing the structure for an interaction involves breaking the content down into a series of clearly defined sections, or agenda items, which progress in an orderly fashion towards the desired outcome. The content needs to be described in outline at the beginning of the interaction, as if you were the navigator explaining to your driver the route you were going to follow. For example:

> OK, Carrie. Why don't you give me the background to the situation with Max. Then I'd like to help you review the causes of the present problem; then we can look at the options you've identified and see if there are any others; and by the end you should be able to decide on a way forward yourself.

People appreciate having an understanding of how the discussion will get them to where they want to go. It reassures them that they will reach their destination and helps them prepare for the demands of the journey by giving them clear expectations about what will happen.

In the example, I was **giving directions** to Carrie, and this is a form of behaviour which is extremely effective at providing structure in interactions. It should be used throughout the discussion, in the same way that when you get to the M62 you might explain to the driver in more detail what is involved in the next stage of the journey (sitting in a traffic jam for long periods). You should start each new section with more directions, both to remind the other person of what happens next and to provide more detail – you may even need to change direction according to what is happening (e.g. to avoid the traffic jams . . .). For example:

> Carrie, before we move on to considering options for the specific problem with Max, I think we should spend a few minutes looking at ways in which we can avoid similar problems occurring in the future. I'd like you to suggest steps that you could take to reduce the risk of things going wrong.

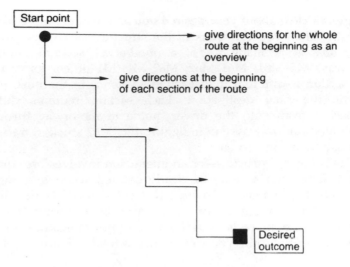

**Figure 9.1** Giving directions

Figure 9.1 illustrates the role of giving directions in structuring an interaction; Skills activity 9.1 gives you a chance to practise.

## SKILLS ACTIVITY 9.1: STRUCTURING

Identify one interaction in the last week which would have been more successful if there had been more structure. 'Map out' the structure you think should have been used by dividing the content into sections and then script how you could have given directions at the beginning to describe the structure you would have liked the discussion to follow.

## Summarizing

When you give directions, you are acting as a signpost, telling the other person where you are going next. The other behaviour that will help you to maintain clarity will be to **summarize** where you have just been. As well as pointing out the route ahead, you are also clarifying the ground that has just been covered. The use of giving directions and summarizing together, to link the various sections of the agenda, will help you to ensure that the structure is maintained throughout the discussion. For example:

We've discussed three options for handling Max: you could ignore him; or you could confront him directly; or I could have a word with him. We've agreed that you are going to have to confront him. What I think we should do now is plan in some detail the best way to do that.

## EXERCISE 9.2

Spend a few minutes now reflecting on the extent to which you use summaries during an interaction to help ensure clarity. Focus on one or two recent discussions which lasted for longer than fifteen minutes. Can you remember whether you or someone else summarized at any point in those discussions? Would the interaction have been clearer if there had been more summarizing?

Some people do use summaries naturally and frequently. Others do not use them at all – they are not part of the behavioural repertoire. People tend to know that they should summarize at the *end* of a discussion, but do not use summarizing as a structuring behaviour during a discussion. I am a great fan of the summary – it is a very valuable behaviour and one that is well worth having as part of your behavioural toolkit. It has many uses, but it is of particular value in structuring discussions, because it:

- Slows the meeting down and gives you time to think.
- Consolidates the ground that has been covered.
- Provides an opportunity to review the structure and make changes if necessary.
- Ensures that there is shared understanding throughout the discussion.

Figure 9.2 (overleaf) illustrates how giving directions and summarizing combine to provide structure to an interaction.

## Handling diversions

**Giving directions** and **summarizing** are the two key behaviours for controlling the structure of an interaction. We have seen how they act as signposts which mark out the key stages of the agreed route. They can also be used to control unwelcome diversions (the driver knows this great little shortcut which will avoid all the traffic!). Diversions are one of the great threats to a discussion: they disrupt the structure, throw things out of sequence and can generate

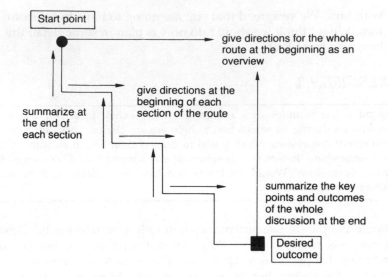

**Figure 9.2** Directions and summarizing

considerable confusion. They can cause you to lose sight of where you are trying to get to, and thus make it much more difficult to get there. Exercise 9.3 will help you to connect this to your own experience.

## EXERCISE 9.3

Spend a few minutes now reflecting on times when you have been discussing someone's performance with them and they have tried to divert the course of the conversation. Do you feel you handle such diversions effectively, or do they tend to disrupt the structure of the discussion?

The diversion represents a struggle over who is in control of the agenda. In that sense, it is a *process* issue, and should be regarded as such. The mistake we often make is to treat it as a content issue, and to allow ourselves to get sucked into discussing the substance of the diversion. It is at that moment that we lose control of the interaction. Case study 9.2 is an example of how it can go wrong.

## CASE STUDY 9.2

*Carrie:*    I admit that I haven't handled him very well, but the real problem is Max. Everybody knows he's out of his depth and Sally lets him get away with it. Why should I have to confront him when she doesn't?

*Hank:*    You think Sally isn't doing anything?

*Carrie:*    Well, if she is doing something, it isn't working, is it?

The mistake has been made: I have engaged fatally in the content of Carrie's diversion. There may be some truth in what she is saying. There may even be some value in discussing it further – but *not now.* Case study 9.3 shows how giving directions and summarizing can be used to get the conversation back on track.

## CASE STUDY 9.3

*Carrie:*    I admit that I haven't handled him very well, but the real problem is Max. Everybody knows he's out of his depth, and Sally lets him get away with it. Why should I have to confront him when she doesn't?

*Hank:*    OK Carrie, you recognize that you could handle Max better and we also know that Max is a difficult customer. I think it's going to be more useful for us to focus on what *you* can do to avoid problems in the future. I don't think it's appropriate for me to discuss Sally's management style with you. Let's look at what steps you could take the next time you need Max's co-operation.

Summarizing is being used in this case study to trace the diversion back to its source – to literally return the conversation to the point from which I want it to continue – as a preface to giving firm directions to move it forward. There is also an acknowledgement of the diversion which clearly indicates my reaction to it and shows Carrie that I do not want to discuss it. This is to stop her trying to make the same diversion again later in the discussion. We will look in more detail at the need to react clearly later in this chapter. Use Skills activity 9.2 to begin to learn how you could handle such situations better.

## *SKILLS ACTIVITY 9.2: HANDLING DIVERSIONS*

Identify one interaction which was badly disrupted because the other person made a diversion. Use summarizing and giving directions to script what you could have said at the point of diversion to retain control of the discussion.

To summarize, before moving on:

- Give an overview of the structure of the interaction before you start.
- Summarize at the end of each section of the structure to consolidate progress and ensure agreement.
- Give specific directions at the beginning of each section which clarify what is required of each person.
- Use the combination of summarizing and giving directions to control any attempts to divert the discussion from the planned route.
- Summarize at the end the main points that have been discussed and agreed.

### Focusing the discussion

The basic structuring behaviour that has just been outlined applies to all kinds of interaction, whether an appraisal interview or a team meeting, and to all kinds of subject matter. There are times, however, particularly with people-management issues, when more elaborate structuring is required in order to focus the discussion on the issues that you want to address.

This became vividly clear to me when I listened to how appraisers tended to start a discussion about an aspect of someone's performance. They created several problems for themselves because of what they said and did not say. Case study 9.4 is a crude illustration, but in my experience, it is very typical. Use Exercise 9.4 to consider the extent to which it reflects what you tend to do in appraisals.

## *CASE STUDY 9.4*

*Appraiser:*    Let's look at time management now. How do you feel you managed your time overall last year?

| *Appraisee:* | I thought I did OK. |
| *Appraiser:* | (who doesn't think appraisee did OK at all) Why do you think that? |
| *Appraisee:* | (who is becoming suspicious) Why, do you think there was a problem with my time management? |
| *Appraiser:* | No. Well. Do you think you – – ? |

## EXERCISE 9.4

Spend a few minutes now reflecting on whether the scenario above bears any resemblance to the way you would start a discussion about an area of performance during an appraisal. If it is, has this caused you problems when the appraisee has not shared your perception about the performance issue? If it is not, how do you typically start such discussions?

The kind of opening in Case study 9.4 is likely to lead to difficulty because it fails to focus the discussion on what the appraiser really wants to talk about: the problems with the appraisee's time management. It generates an uncomfortable dance around the issue, in which neither party is saying what they really think. Much time can be wasted as a result and the climate of the interaction can be damaged. To avoid this trap, people need to focus the discussion clearly from the beginning so that they can ask questions which get to the root of the issue. The following process, called 'creating a platform', will help you to do this.

## Creating a platform

There are three stages in creating a platform. The first is to establish a positive **purpose**. It is a feature of dealing with difficult performance issues that we tend to initiate a discussion of the issue without explaining, in broad terms, what we are hoping to achieve. In most cases, we discuss performance problems with people because we want to help them to improve. This purpose is often not made clear and the discussion suffers as a result.

The purpose you establish should be one that will not engender disagreement or resistance. It needs to be:

- A **general** statement of intent – not, for example, a specific outcome or solution.

- A **positive** statement which is clearly in the interests of the other person.

For example: 'I want to discuss time management with you so that we can make sure that you are handling your work in the most efficient way and not overloading yourself.' A statement like this provides a positive context for any criticism that you may need to make and will probably generate some commitment to working constructively together on the issue.

The second stage is clarifying your **position**. Because appraisers do not usually like giving negative feedback, they often hope that the appraisee will 'confess' weakness so that they do not have to be openly critical. Appraisees are rarely so obliging, especially if their salary increase is at stake! The main cause of the difficulty in the scenario illustrated above is that the appraiser is not being clear about his position on the performance issue being addressed. He is critical of the appraisee's time management, but he is not saying so, and so is likely to do one or all of the following:

- Fail to give the discussion a specific focus.

- Trap himself into arguing about *whether* there is a problem rather than focusing on *why* there is a problem.

- Make the impact of the criticism worse when it finally comes.

You will make life much easier for yourself if you clarify your position early by giving some feedback about your perception of the issue. For example: 'I am concerned about how hard you are working at the moment, and I am worried that you will burn yourself out if you are not careful.' 'I am unhappy with the way you set priorities and the impact that that has on you getting your work in on time.' Note that in both examples, the behaviour used is the same as that described in the chapter on climate for modelling openness. By describing your feelings ('concerned', 'unhappy') you are softening the criticism so that it is more acceptable to the other person.

Clarifying your position in this way may feel risky. In fact, it is less risky than not doing so. By stating your concern, you have made it clear that there is an issue that needs addressing. You may need to give some details to substantiate your concerns. But the fact is, if you think there is a problem, then there *is* a problem. The discussion can now focus on how to tackle that issue, without having to establish whether the issue exists.

When you have clarified your position, you will be able to establish an appropriate **structure** for the discussion, in the ways described in the previous section of this chapter. Here is an example of the kind of structure that you may need to set up to review the appraisee's time management:

> What I want to do is look at how you set priorities at the moment. Then we can review the impact of those priorities on your work and assess whether they need to change, and if so how. I'd like to finish by agreeing a clear set of priorities for the next three months and then planning how you can use them to help you manage your workload.

A structure like this enables you to focus on the issue in a specific and productive way. The three stages together will take less than two minutes to say, but could save you many minutes of fruitless discussion. Here they are:

> I want to discuss time management with you so that we can make sure that you are handling your workload in the most efficient way and not overloading yourself. I am concerned about the way you set priorities and the impact that that has on you getting your work in on time. What I want to do is look at how you set priorities at the moment. Then we can review the impact of those priorities on your work and assess whether they need to change, and if so how. I'd like to finish by agreeing a clear set of priorities for the next three months and then planning how you can use them to help you manage your workload.

## Applications of the platform

Creating a platform is a type of structuring that is particularly useful when tackling poor performance issues in appraisals. Having said that, it is also useful when tackling most performance issues in formal or informal interactions. It can be used to address positive performance issues in appraisals and to structure informal coaching discussions. Here are some examples of how the tool can be used in different situations.

The positive performance issue:

- Position: I'm very pleased with the way you've handled customer inquiries and complaints and I'm hoping to hand over more of that kind of work to you next year.
- Purpose: I'd like to spend some time discussing the impact that this might have on the rest of your work so that we make sure we're not creating any problems for ourselves.

- Structure: Let's start by reviewing the calls that you've handled so far and see whether you've had any problems with those. Then we can look at the work that you've got coming in and see what demands that will make on your time. Then if it's possible we could look at you taking on responsibility for certain accounts.

The coaching discussion:

- Purpose: I want to review how things are going with Max so that we ensure we're getting a better service from him.
- Position: I'm a bit disappointed that things haven't improved since we last spoke and would like to get to the bottom of why that is.
- Structure: Can we start by summarizing the steps that you said you'd take and then find out whether you did take them and, if you did, what happened. If you didn't, we need to sort out why. If necessary, we will have to identify an alternative course of action.

To summarize 'creating a platform', before moving on:

- Establish a positive **purpose** for the discussion.
- Clarify your **position** by giving feedback.
- Then establish an appropriate **structure**.

## SKILLS ACTIVITY 9.3: CREATING A PLATFORM

Identify a discussion that you need to have with one of the people you manage about their performance in the near future. Think through how you could use 'creating a platform' to provide a focused starting point for the interaction. Then write a script of what you could say to create such a platform.

In this section we have looked at some of the general principles of structuring interactions in order to ensure clarity. We will look at different types of structure to achieve particular outcomes in later chapters, specifically: structures for reviewing performance and learning experiences in Chapter 10 on content; structures for problem-solving and persuading in Chapter 11 on commitment.

---

# Seeking clarification

---

Effective structuring in the ways described above will help you to ensure that the *process* of the interaction is clear to those involved. We can now look at how you can ensure that you both share the same understanding concerning the *content* of the interaction.

You will partly achieve this if you summarize at the end of each section of the structure you have established. This will give you the opportunity to check your own understanding and to see if the other person agrees with it. There will be times, however, during a section of the discussion when you will need to clarify the meaning of what the other person is saying, either to help your own or the other person's understanding.

It is important at these times that you seek clarification, using questions which will ensure that a shared understanding is reached, like the following:

- **Do you mean** that Max knows what you want but doesn't co-operate, or that he doesn't know what you want?
- **Are you saying** the Max never co-operates with anybody?
- **So you think** that confronting Max with the problem is likely to make things worse?

Questions like these are one of the indicators of an effective communicator, because they demonstrate good listening skills. They show the other person that you have heard what they have said and are keen to understand it better. This has a positive impact on the climate of the interaction, and helps to unravel the confusion that commonly creeps into discussions and the ambiguities of meaning that can arise (see Skills activity 9.4). In the examples above, they are moving Carrie into a deeper and more specific analysis of her problems with Max. They are serving as 'second-level' questions, getting behind the surface presentation of the situation.

## *SKILLS ACTIVITY 9.4: SEEKING CLARIFICATION*

Identify a discussion that you have had recently which would have gone better if you had sought more clarification from the other person. Write down five questions, like the ones in the examples above, which, if you had asked them, would have improved the clarity and quality of the interaction.

Questions which seek clarification have a number of uses over and above their primary one of providing clarity. It is this combination of uses that give them such an important role to play in interactions concerning people management. Here are three other ways of using them:

- To encourage the person to think more deeply, for example: 'Are you saying that you should go to the top of Max's priorities when you need something from him?'

- To challenge perceptions, for example: 'Do you really mean that the way you behave doesn't make any difference to Max's response?'

- To signal disagreement with proposals, for example: 'Do you think that Max is going to feel better about you if I've had to speak to him about the situation?'

Used in this way, these questions are powerful interactive tools which will help you to control the discussion and influence the perceptions of the other person.

---

# Reacting clearly

---

There are two sides to the issue of clarity in people-management interactions. On the one hand, you want to understand what other people are saying; on the other, they want to understand your **reaction** to what they are saying. Asking questions will help you to achieve the first, but may well create difficulties with the second, because when we use a high questioning style, this often has the effect of lowering our reacting level. We are concentrating so much on what questions to ask that we forget to react clearly to the answers we are getting. Low reacting can generate doubt and anxiety in the receiver and so have a negative impact on the climate of the interaction.

Responding clearly has a positive impact on the clarity of an interaction as well as the climate. I have covered the general principles of responding behaviour in Chapter 8. In this chapter, I am going to focus on one aspect in more detail – disagreeing behaviour. It is often our reluctance to disagree, or our inability to disagree clearly enough, that causes us problems with the clarity of our communication with our people.

We have seen that, as long as you have a balance of reacting behaviour, there is no reason not to disagree – it will not be perceived as negative and may even be greeted with relief. On the other hand, there are some very good reasons why you *should* disagree, clearly and firmly, in people-management interactions.

## Challenging self-perception

When the other person presents you with a self-perception that you disagree with, it can be useful for you to state your disagreement early so that you can focus the discussion more constructively. For example:

*Appraisee:* I feel that I'm ready to take on a more active role with the customers.

*Appraiser:* I don't think you're ready quite yet, but I'd like to look at what we need to do to get you to a place where you are.

*Appraisee:* I haven't got the self-confidence to go and see customers on my own.

*Appraiser:* I'm not sure that self-confidence is the problem. I'd like to look more specifically at what worries you about doing it.

## Controlling diversions

When we looked at structuring earlier in this chapter, there was an example (see p. 171) of the need to disagree in order to control a diversion. Clear disagreement is vital to show that you do not intend to engage with the diversion. For example:

*Appraisee:* Marie lets Curt go with her on customer visits and he's been in the company less time than me.

*Appraiser:* I don't think that length of service is relevant here. I want to focus on the skills required in relating to customers.

## Stopping fruitless argument

When discussing an issue, you can sometimes find yourself locked in an argument or debate which, although relevant, will get you both nowhere slowly! It is difficult to extract yourself from these fruitless debates – the key is to use clear disagreement to signal that the argument is not going to continue. For example:

*Appraisee:*　　I don't think it's us, I think it's the sales people – they don't care about the problems they create as long as they get their bonus and if I go out with them they don't want me to say anything to the customer in case I blow the sale, so I think you're being a bit unfair focusing on the engineers.

*Appraiser:*　　I'm not focusing on the engineers, and I'm not taking sides with the sales people. I want to look at how you could manage your relationship with Frank to avoid the problems you've been talking about.

In all four of these examples, clear disagreement, stated early, will enable you to control the interaction so that it focuses on the issues you want to discuss. If it is balanced by times when you agree it will not have a negative impact on the climate, even though the other person may not share your opinion. And it is likely to save you a lot of time. In each case, control is achieved firstly by **disagreeing** clearly and secondly by **giving directions**. This combination is important because it:

- Denies the other person the time to challenge your disagreement.
- Provides a positive way forward for discussing the issue.

## SKILLS ACTIVITY 9.5: DISAGREEING CLEARLY

> Identify a discussion that you have had recently which would have gone better if you had disagreed clearly with the other person. Write down what you could have said, using disagreeing and giving directions behaviours, to show disagreement and redirect the discussion in a positive direction.

Many people feel uncomfortable about disagreeing and tend to avoid doing so for fear that it will provoke a negative response. You may have felt that you could not have disagreed in the ways illustrated in the examples and so find Skills activity 9.5 difficult to do. If this is the case, my advice is to practise, first by rehearsing disagreements that you would like to have made and second, by actually disagreeing in low-risk interactions. You will probably find that your disagreements do not provoke the response that you fear – often quite the opposite.

---

# Summary: providing clarity

---

In this chapter we have looked at three aspects of providing clarity in discussions about performance.

## Structuring

- Establish the structure for the discussion at the beginning by: dividing the content into sections and giving an overview of the 'route' the discussion will take.
- Manage the structure throughout the discussion by summarizing at the end of each section and giving specific directions at the beginning of each section.
- Where appropriate, create a platform for your questions at the beginning of a discussion by establishing a positive purpose; clarifying your position; and establishing the structure.

## Seeking clarification

- Use questions to ensure that there is mutual understanding. These opening words will help you frame such questions: 'Do you mean . . .?' 'Are you saying . . .?' 'So you think . . .?'
- Use these questions also to: encourage deeper analysis; challenge perceptions and opinions; and disagree with ideas and proposals.

## Reacting clearly

- Express your agreement and disagreement so that the other people are clear about how you are reacting to what they are saying.

- Don't be afraid to disagree when appropriate. Disagreement is a valuable behaviour which can usefully challenge inaccurate self-perceptions; control diversionary tactics; stop fruitless arguments.

End this chapter by doing Skills activity 9.6, which gives you a structure for practising the skills of ensuring clarity.

## SKILLS ACTIVITY 9.6: CLARITY

Identify a suitable opportunity for you to practise the lessons from this chapter. This will ideally be a semi-formal or informal discussion with one of your people about an aspect of their performance. Before you meet them, plan how you are going to ensure that you maintain clarity throughout the interaction. Decide the following:

- How you are going to establish an appropriate structure for the discussion.
- Whether you need to create a platform in order to focus the interaction on the issues you want to discuss.
- How you can ensure that you use summaries and giving direction to maintain structure and clarity throughout the discussion.
- How you can ensure that you use seeking clarification and disagreeing behaviour to increase the understanding of issues and perspectives throughout the discussion.

# 10

# Content

So far in Part 3, we have looked at the skills involved in managing the *process* of an interaction by focusing on issues of climate and clarity. It is now time to look at how to manage the *content* of the interaction. This and the next two chapters will focus on how to manage the content in order to achieve your desired outcomes. In this chapter, we will look at the basic requirements for the effective management of most people-management discussions.

There are two main kinds of contact that you have with the people you manage. You interact with them:

- Before they do something, for example, setting objectives, delegating responsibilities, explaining tasks, planning activities.
- After they do something, for example, reviewing overall performance, monitoring progress, reviewing experiences and activities, consolidating learning, giving feedback, identifying areas for improvement.

We shall concentrate on the second of these two types of interaction, for the following reasons:

- The work we have already done, both in Part 2 on planning and so far in Part 3 will help you with the 'before' interactions.
- The 'after' interactions tend to be more difficult to manage.
- Some of the lessons that will arise from focusing on 'after' interactions will be directly applicable to 'before' interactions.

Specifically, we shall be exploring the following:

- The **principles** that underpin reviewing performance and giving feedback.
- The **structure** you need to establish to ensure that your desired outcome is achieved.
- The **skills** required to manage the interaction effectively.

The work that you will be doing in this chapter refers back to and builds on the ground covered in Chapters 8 and 9. For example, in Chapter 9, we looked at the skills involved in establishing structures; in this chapter we shall look in detail at the kind of structures you need to establish. You will find it easier to work through this chapter if you have already read the previous two.

---

# Principles

---

One of the key choices you have to make about the people you manage concerns the extent to which you focus on managing their activity or developing their performance. This is a choice that you make each time you sit down with one of your people to review an activity or a period of time (use Exercise 10.1 to think about this). You have to decide on the *function* of the interaction.

## *EXERCISE 10.1*

> Spend a few minutes now reflecting on what purpose you give to the time you spend reviewing work with your people. Do you regard this as coaching time, with the focus on learning and development? Or do you regard this as management time, with the focus on monitoring activity?

In my experience, most managers tend to use the time they give over to reviewing on managing activity rather than developing performance. We have seen that this is appropriate with people who do not have the potential or motivation to improve their performance (see Chapter 6). With others, however, it will be missing out on an opportunity to help them develop. The richest source of learning that we have is our experiences at work. When you are coaching somebody, one of your main contributions is to make sure that he or she learns from that experience.

In this chapter, therefore, we shall focus on managing review discussions which are aimed at developing performance. Before we start looking in detail at structures and skills, I want to establish some underlying principles which form the context for such interactions. These are as follows:

- **Purpose:** The purpose behind the reviewing time you spend with your people should be **to help them to learn from their experience in order to improve their performance**.

- **Timing:** The contact should take place as soon after the activity or experience being reviewed as possible, so that it can be remembered and referred to clearly and accurately.

- **Focus:** The interaction should focus on those issues concerning the activity or experience which will help people identify achievable next steps to improve their performance.

- **Accuracy:** The review should be based on a factual account of what happened, so that the analysis that follows can accurately identify the key learning issues.

- **Action:** The contact should result in clearly identified and agreed actions which the other person can take in order to improve performance.

The last three of these principles involve skills that we will look at in detail later on. The first two are more to do with your attitude to performance management and need to be dealt with here briefly.

## Purpose

It is important to recognize that every contact you have with your people is a potential coaching interaction. It is up to you whether you spot the opportunity and decide to make use of it. This is particularly true when you are monitoring or reviewing work: you can regard this as simply a management activity in which you, for example, reassure yourself that things are getting done on time; or you can use it as an opportunity to ensure that your people are learning from their experience and thinking about how they can apply that learning in the future. Do Exercise 10.2 to think through how you could best use contact with your people.

## EXERCISE 10.2

> Spend a few minutes now reflecting on the opportunities you will have
> in the near future to review activity with some of the people you
> manage. Decide whether these are opportunities to develop the people's
> performance, or whether it is more appropriate to use them to manage
> activity.

A review discussion which focuses on learning and performance
will be different from one that focuses on monitoring and activity.
So it is important for you to clarify what your purpose is each time
you sit down with one of your people to review their work. You
need to ask yourself: am I going to use this as a coaching
opportunity?

## Timing

The timing of your reviewing and its proximity to the activity or
experience being reviewed will depend on the extent to which you
have built such contact with your staff into your on-going process
for managing them. If you have not read Chapter 4, which deals
with this issue, it may be worth you reading it now or when you
have finished this chapter.

If your purpose is to help somebody to develop their performance, reviewing is likely to be one of your key contributions. Having
said that, it is not always easy to review things in time. When I was
developing training consultants, there were times when it was
literally impossible – we were away from the office so much that we
could not fix times to meet. In such circumstances, it is probably
better for the review not to take place: too much will have happened
in between, memories will become blurred, other issues become
more pressing.

So, whenever possible:

- Have regular review meetings in which general performance
  issues can be reviewed.

- Schedule review meetings into the timetable for a specific
  learning activity. For example, if you are sending people on
  training programmes, schedule meetings with them before they
  go and when they come back.

- If an opportunity to review something crops up unexpectedly,
  make the time to do it properly. You might not be able to do this

immediately – it may be better to arrange a time in the near future when you can give the review your full attention.

## *EXERCISE 10.3*

Spend a few minutes now reflecting on the opportunities you had to review a piece of work with one of your people over the last month. Did you build review discussions into planned activity? Did you respond positively to unexpected opportunities?

---

# Structure

---

Whether the purpose of your 'after' contact is to monitor activity or develop performance, the interaction needs to be structured carefully if it is to be successful. The rest of this chapter is built around a basic structure that you can apply to almost every review discussion which you are using to help people learn from their experience. With minor modification, it can also be applied to discussions in which you are managing activity. It is this:

1. Gather an accurate picture of what happened.
2. Register and consolidate what went well.
3. Identify where things went wrong.
4. Analyze why things went wrong.
5. Prioritize areas for learning.
6. Develop an action plan.

This structure provides a clear and logical path for a review discussion. It acts as a funnel, channelling the discussion towards a specific and realistic plan of action which will lead to improved performance. There are some aspects of the structure that need to be explored in more detail. These are:

- Starting-points.
- Balance.
- Overload.
- Timing of solutions.

## Starting-points

The key to using the structure successfully is to start at the right place. I will use an example from my own experience to show that this can be more difficult than it sounds.

There is one training programme I have run which stands out in my mind as an absolute disaster. This was because one of the participants, the Human Resources Director of the company, my client, behaved appallingly throughout. He walked out in the middle of a feedback session. He turned up late in the mornings. He stared out of the window during inputs. He tore up handouts in front of the whole group, in the middle of a session. To put it mildly – he did not hide his dissatisfaction with the programme!

I have spent a lot of time thinking about that experience, focusing on how I should have handled the situation – the things I could have said, the stand I could have taken. But, frankly, this reflection has not been that useful. It is unlikely that I am going to come across somebody behaving in such a destructive way again.

A colleague helped me to see that it would be more useful for me to focus on reviewing *why* I had got into that situation in the first place. I knew this man's reputation – I had been warned about him by his subordinates! Was it wise for him to have been on the programme in the first place? Taking it further back: I knew that the programme did not meet all the client's expressed needs. I felt it met people's real needs and wanted to prove it through their experiencing the programme. Was that wise? Could I have managed the selling process more effectively? This was a far more fruitful area for review, for two reasons: I come across such problems all the time in my selling activity; and it would help me to avoid the situation that so upset me.

I started reviewing that experience by focusing on the part of it that had most impact on me – the behaviour of the HR Director on the programme. This is often where people want to start: with the extreme points of the experience – what went really badly or really well. Although these points need to be dealt with, they are not necessarily the best places to start, for the following reasons:

- They can dominate the discussion.
- They are not necessarily the areas from which the most useful learning will be derived.
- They have an emotional charge that will make it difficult for the person to review the experience calmly and rationally.

## EXERCISE 10.4

> Spend a few minutes now reflecting on one or two times when you have helped someone to review an experience. Did the review start at the most appropriate point? Would it have been more effective if it had started at another point? Did you discuss how to start reviewing the experience, or did it happen automatically?

In order to identify the most appropriate starting point for a review discussion, as you are asked to in Exercise 10.4, it helps to:

● **Summarize the key stages of the experience.** For example, if you are helping somebody review how he or she managed a team meeting, the key stages might be: deciding the agenda, communicating the agenda, planning for the meeting, starting the meeting, managing the process, recording the outcomes.

● **Decide where the most useful starting point will be.** The problems experienced in the meeting may be the result of a poor agenda or lack of preparation, for example.

## Balance

When we help people review their experience, we tend to focus on the problems they have had, the mistakes they have made, and the weak areas of their performance. It is likely that this is where the most useful learning will come from, so it is sensible to invest our time and effort here. The trouble is that we often forget to spend any time registering what went well and ensuring that those successes are repeated in the future. There are two downsides to this:

● It can be dispiriting – the focus on problems, although useful, can leave us feeling that we do not get anything right!
● It can be wasteful – there is as much potential learning from our successes as there is from our failings.

That is why the second stage of the structure is to:

● **Register** what went well by spending time identifying successes and making sure that you both acknowledge them as strengths in the person's performance.

- **Consolidate** successes by ensuring that the person understands why they went well and is able to achieve them again in the future.

## Overload

Another common mistake that we make when we review things with people is that we try to do too much. People can only learn so much at any one time – and more importantly, they are probably able to apply even less. If you want your review discussions to lead to positive action, you need to make sure that you do not *overload* your learners with potential learning. You need to prioritize the key points that will enable them to take achievable next steps to improved performance.

This is why the structure is shaped like a funnel (p. 187). And it is why the key word at the fifth stage of the structure is **prioritize** areas for learning. You may uncover several areas for potential learning during the earlier stages of the discussion. At the fifth stage, you must decide the following:

- How many of these learners will realistically be able to manage, i.e. how many learning points will they be able to retain and apply to their work? As a rule of thumb, I would recommend you should prioritize no more than three issues at this stage. It may be fewer, depending on the complexity of the issues, the competence and self-confidence of the individual learner, and the time that you have available.

- Which areas to focus on. These will not necessarily be the most important ones in your view. They are the ones that provide the next best steps in terms of learners' development, i.e. learning which builds on their existing knowledge and skills, and which they will be able to put into practice.

Use Exercise 10.5 to consider the extent to which you make these decisions when you are reviewing your people's work with them.

Overload is one of my weak areas as a coach. When, for example, I am helping a trainer review a session that I have just watched them deliver, I have usually noted down a long list of learning points. I want to address them all and have often overwhelmed people with the volume of my feedback. It is not that the points I want to make are not valuable, but they do not *all* have to be dealt with there and then. Sometimes trainers will sort things out for themselves without

## EXERCISE 10.5

> Spend a few minutes now reflecting on the degree to which you try to achieve too much in your review discussions. Are you in danger of overloading the other person by focusing on too many issues or learning points? Would your reviews be more effective if you prioritized the points you felt needed addressing in terms of the best next learning steps?

me saying anything. Or the issue will crop up again later, at a time when people are in a better place to tackle it. I will be of much more help if I prioritize the two or three key points which will move learners one step forward, than address ten points which leave them feeling like abject failures.

## Timing of solutions

The final point about the structure is that it is designed to stop you from coming up with solutions too early. In many of the review discussions that I observe, managers are keen to help people resolve problems that they are experiencing. As soon as problems have been expressed or identified, the manager will suggest ways of tackling them, or ask the other people to come up with their own ideas. It is important that reviews are positive and action oriented, but if the purpose of the review is to help someone learn from their experience, it is equally important that you do not move into the solution phase before the person has had a chance to reflect on the nature and causes of the problem. There are two reasons for this:

- Much can be learnt from an exploration of the nature and causes of the problems someone is experiencing.
- You are more likely to come up with a good-quality solution if you have analyzed the causes of the problem first.

## EXERCISE 10.6

> Spend a few minutes reflecting on the extent to which you jump into solution-giving mode when you are helping people to review their experience. Do you tend to suggest solutions as soon as a problem has been expressed? Or do you explore the problem more fully before helping the other person to identify a way forward?

If Exercise 10.6 has shown you that you dive into solutions too early, the reviewing structure will help you to stop doing so, because it asks you to analyze why things went wrong and prioritize areas for learning first. This may require some self-discipline on your part. The tendency to dive into solutions, like the tendency to dive into content, can be hard to control. Part of the problem is that you probably do know the answer – and it will so obviously be of help. But although giving the answer may solve the immediate problem, it will not necessarily help the person to learn for the future.

## SKILLS ACTIVITY 10.1: STRUCTURING A REVIEW

> Identify an opportunity to practise reviewing with one of your people. This should be an activity or experience at which you were present, or at least have first-hand data about what happened and how they performed. Ideally, there should be both areas of good performance and problems or difficulties to be reviewed.
>
> Use the structure above to plan your review in detail, making notes at each stage for issues you could discuss and the best ways to discuss them. Pay particular emphasis to:
>
> - Starting-points.
> - Balance.
> - Overload.
> - Timing of solutions.

You may have found that you could not plan the review in Skills activity 10.1 in much detail because you could not anticipate the issues that needed discussing until you spoke to the other person. Or you may have found that you had to adapt the structure to fit the particular requirements of the situation. The purpose of the exercise was to start you thinking about how you can structure review discussions so that you use them to help people learn from their experience. I hope, even if it has been difficult for practical reasons, that it has achieved that aim.

# Skills

Having established the structure for effective reviewing, we shall now look at the behavioural skills involved in using that structure. We shall go through each of the six stages in turn and examine the skills required to manage that stage effectively.

## Gather an accurate picture of what happened

The kind of work you need to do at this first stage will be slightly different depending on whether you were present during the event you are reviewing or not. If, for example, you accompanied an engineer on a client visit, you will have your own first-hand account of what happened, which you can use during the review. If, on the other hand, you are reviewing a client visit which the engineer made on his own, you will have no first-hand data of your own and will be dependent on the learner's version of events.

With both scenarios, however, your role is to help the learner to reconstruct an *objective* account of the experience. There are two key points to bear in mind:

- You should generate as full and accurate an account of what happened as possible **before** you start evaluating it.
- The information you gather must be as factual and specific as possible.

The main behaviour you will be using is questioning and the questions you ask must seek **specific** information. I cannot stress the importance of this enough. People often relate their experiences in ways that make effective reviewing difficult. They may talk in generalizations; they may use vague or abstract language; their emotions may distort their perspective; they may remember things inaccurately. By seeking specific information, you can help them to become more objective about the event at the same time as constructing an accurate picture. The golden rule is: **ask for details**.

In their simplest form, the questions you use to gather an accurate picture of what happened are 'what' questions. For example:

- **What** happened when you asked Max to give you the figures you needed?

- **What** reasons did Max give for why he could not get the figures together in time?
- **What** was your reaction when he said that?

'What' questions are a good place to start when gathering data. As the picture starts to form, you will have to ask a broad range of questions to get the right level of detail. Here are five sorts of detail that you may need to gather, with examples of appropriate questions.

### Illustration

If the people you are coaching tend to talk about themselves and their performance in broad or abstract terms, it can be hard to understand exactly what they mean and difficult to deal with the issue constructively. For example, a person who feels inadequate in writing skills, might say: 'I'm just not very good at writing. I don't write very well. It takes me for ever to do it and it ends up being pretty dreadful anyway.'

When people describe a problem in this way, you first need to *substantiate* what they are saying. One way of doing this is to ask them to illustrate the issue with a specific example or case study, using questions like: 'Has there been a report you've written recently that you weren't happy with?' 'Can you give me an example of a piece of writing that you felt took you too long to write?' 'Are you thinking of the report you wrote on the tests you did last week?'

### Scale

Illustration will help you to establish whether the self-analysis is accurate. Having done that, you may need to explore the *scale* of the issue, in order to help the learner to keep it in perspective. We often generalize about ourselves, using one or two powerful experiences, good or bad, as the basis for a fully formed self-image. For example: 'It always takes me for ages to write those reports and I never feel that I do my work justice.' Words like 'never' and 'always' are tip-offs that you need to work on scale.

You need to establish the true scale, not just to help the learner gain perspective, but to make it possible to work constructively on the issue together. Questions like these will be useful: 'Does *all* your writing take too long, or are there some things that you can write quite quickly?' 'Is it true that *all* your reports aren't any good, or is it just some of them that you're not happy with?' 'Have there been any reports you have written that you felt did reflect the quality of your work?'

## Chronology

People often retain an event or experience in their memory as a series of highlights. These are selected because they have had the most impact. When I remember a football game, for example, I remember the goals first, then the chances that were missed or the dramatic saves. I do not necessarily remember these in the right sequence: I order them in terms of their dramatic value. The same principle applies to events at work: you tend to recall most easily the things that went really well or really badly, and these are the ones you want to concentrate on if you are reviewing the event, either on your own or with someone else.

If you are being given a jumble of edited highlights, it will help if you can establish an exact chronology for what happened. This will help the person to slow down and get a more detached perspective. You can do this by asking questions like: 'Did you get a clear briefing from Jack about how he intended to use the report?' 'What was the first thing you did when you sat down to start writing the report?' 'How did you go about planning the structure?' 'What did you do once you'd written down the main headings for the report?'

## Script

Our memories can be very self-serving: they can quietly reconstruct what actually happened so that it better serves the picture we would like to have of the event and of ourselves. One of the ways it does this is to blur details and focus on moods. This is particularly true when dealing with other people's responses to us. If it suits our emotional needs to believe that they loved us, hated us, thought we were useless, were impressed with our brilliance, our memories will filter their actual responses so that they fit our desired self-image.

If the person you are helping is presenting you with a vague and generalized account of how other people responded – 'I could tell Jack wasn't very impressed with it' – you need to bed these impressions down into hard facts. Ask questions like these: 'What did Jack actually say to you when he'd read the report?' 'Did he *say* that he wasn't happy with it?' 'What did Jack *do* that made you feel the report was rubbish?'

## Internal responses

Finally, you may need to gather information about a person's internal responses to their experience. Sometimes the accounts we give of events concentrate on the external factors: what happened, what was said, what the other people did. Accounts like these miss out the way that we processed the experience: our thoughts and feelings as the event unfolded. We are often unaware of what these are, but they can provide vital clues as to why things have gone well or badly.

It is often only when we have understood our inner processes that we are able to manage our responses more effectively. So you may need to encourage people to remember them as part of a review process, using questions like these: 'How did you feel after Jack had briefed you about the report?' 'When you'd mapped out the structure, did you feel happy that that was the right structure for the report?' 'Are you clear about what you want to say before you start writing each section or do you hope it will emerge through the writing?'

## EXERCISE 10.7

Spend a few minutes reflecting on an instance when you helped somebody to review an aspect of their work.

- Do you feel that you gathered a full enough picture at the beginning to provide a basis for the rest of the review?
- Did the effectiveness of the review suffer as a result?
- Would it have helped if you had gathered more data?
- Would any of the five kinds of detail listed above (illustration, scale, chronology, script or internal responses) have been of particular use?

Because of lack of time, and the instinctive desire to focus on problems and solutions, we often do not spend enough time at the beginning of the review piecing together what happened. If the picture we are working from is incomplete, this may lead us to focus on the wrong issues or come up with inappropriate solutions, as you may discover when you do Exercise 10.7. Skills activity 10.2 gives you the opportunity to practise gathering detailed information at the beginning of a review.

## Register and consolidate what went well

Having gathered a full and accurate picture, you can move on to the next stage of the structure: registering and consolidating strengths.

We have established the need and the value of focusing on successes as well as problem areas. There may be times when the

## SKILLS ACTIVITY 10.2: GATHERING DATA

Using the practice opportunity you selected in Skills activity 10.1, plan the questions you need to ask that will help you to gather a full, accurate and objective picture of the subject of the review.

Use your knowledge of the other person to imagine the kind of answers they will give to your questions and plan questions you could ask in response to these answers to get more detail into the picture. You may find it useful to write your plan in the form of a script, in which you write the lines for both you and the other person.

experience or performance was so bad that there is nothing positive to talk about at all. More often, however, we are likely to be reviewing a mix of good and bad performance. Before moving on to the bad, we need to spend some time registering what went well and exploring why it went well, so that strengths are consolidated.

There are three steps to follow at this stage in the review structure:

1. Encourage other people to identify positive aspects of their performance. For example: 'Tell me the aspects of the report that you are most pleased with.' 'What were the sections of the report which you felt worked best?' People often find it difficult to identify or talk about their strengths and may find questions like these hard to answer. It is sometimes important to persevere with them, in order to challenge people's determination to feel bad about themselves!

2. Give feedback about the aspects that you think went well. For example: 'I think the structure you mapped out at the beginning was absolutely right.' 'I'm impressed by the fact that, even though you say it took too long, you still got it to Jack on time.' Only give positive feedback if it is genuine, but if you can identify some positive points in what you have seen or heard, you should make sure that these are acknowledged by the other person.

3. Discuss the positive areas identified in order to consolidate them. For example: 'Tell me how you decided on that structure, given the complexity of the brief Jack gave you.' 'Does identifying the headings for each section help you to stay focused when you start writing?' 'How did you make sure that the report got

finished on time?' Questions like these will help other people to recognize and value their strengths more.

Skills activity 10.3 will help you to practise this.

## *SKILLS ACTIVITY 10.3: REGISTERING STRENGTHS*

Using the practice opportunity you selected in Skills activity 10.1, identify the areas of good performance that you want to recognize and consolidate and then plan how you will do this during the review.

## Identify where things went wrong

Having reinforced the good points, it is time to move on to areas where the person has had difficulties or where there were problems with performance. At this stage, it is just necessary to identify and agree what the problem areas are. This provides the basis for further exploration, and helps you to identify the best agenda for the rest of the discussion.

It is likely that you will have already identified where things went wrong in earlier stages of the review. If that is the case, all that is required is for you to:

- Summarize the key problem areas as you see them from the account that you have been given.
- Check that the other person agrees with your summary.

For example: 'So, from what you've told me, there are three points at which you experience difficulty: keeping to the structure that you have mapped out; identifying what's wrong with your first draft; and adding too much new material when you do the second draft. Is that a fair summary, or have I missed something?'

If you do not feel you have enough information or clarity to summarize the key problem areas, you will need to ask more questions. For example: 'Where do you think things started to go wrong with Jack's report?' 'Is that the only area of difficulty?' 'Can you summarize what you think the key problem areas are for me?' When you have arrived at a clear summary, you will be able to suggest how best to tackle each issue, in terms of sequence and process. If there are several problem areas, it may be necessary to prioritize them at this stage in the review, so that you focus on some areas now, and resolve to look at other issues in another discussion.

## Analyze why things went wrong

Having identified the problem areas to be explored, the next stage is to reach an understanding of the causes of the problem. The temptation at this stage can be to dive into generating solutions to overcome the problems, especially if the solutions seem obvious to you. By resisting this temptation, and helping analyze why things went wrong, the other person may be better able to come up with their own solution, based on a more in-depth understanding of the issues.

In some cases, you may have your own ideas about the causes of the problems and difficulties and will want to use this stage to help the person understand your analysis. In others, you may have no idea and the process of analysis will be of mutual benefit. In both cases, unless you have chosen to use a directing style, the key behaviour will be questioning. Here, however, your questions will be focused on analyzing problems and so will be different from the kind of questions illustrated at earlier stages.

In their simplest form, the questions you use to analyze the causes of problems are 'why' questions. For example: '**Why** do you think you have difficulty keeping to the structure you have mapped out?' '**Why** do you think it takes you so long to write the first draft?' '**Why** do you only get feedback from someone after you had finished the second draft?'

'Why' questions are a good place to start analyzing the causes of problems and difficulties. As the discussion continues, you will need to follow up these questions with others. For example: 'Do you think the structure is detailed enough to provide you with the framework you need?' 'How much time does the first draft take you if you are editing what you write as you go along?' 'When you read the first draft, do you think you focus too much on the content, rather than assessing the structure and clarity?'

### Giving feedback

Questions like these peel back the layers of the onion, providing a fuller and more informed analysis of why things went wrong. There will be times, however, when other people are unable or unwilling to answer your questions at this stage – they may genuinely not know why things went wrong, or be reluctant to accept that what went wrong has anything to do with them. If this happens, you may need to give feedback: *your* opinion of why things went wrong, based on what you have been told or what you saw if you were present during the event.

The danger when you start to give feedback is that you do not stop – you talk at length about your perceptions, opinions and ideas for how things could be improved. You start to dominate discussions rather than control them and, in your desire to help them understand, you lose sight of other people's needs. So, whenever possible, your feedback should be kept to a minimum, and used as a platform for further questions, so that you turn the focus back on to the other person as soon as possible (see Chapter 9 for more information about creating a platform). For example: 'From what you've said, it sounds to me that you are trying too hard to write the perfect report at the first draft. Do you think that is why you edit it as you go along?' 'My feeling is that you are not clear enough before you start writing about the key messages that you want each section to convey. Do you feel you spend enough time on the structure before you start writing?'

Skills activity 10.4 will help you to practise this.

## SKILLS ACTIVITY 10.4: ANALYZING PROBLEMS

> Using the practice opportunity you selected in Skills activity 10.1, plan how you will help the other person to analyze the problems that have arisen in the event that you are reviewing. You may have to imagine that you agree on what these problems are.

The function of the analysis stage is to increase the likelihood of identifying an appropriate solution at the action planning stage. You have to judge how much analysis is required to achieve this. It is possible to spend a long time at the analysis stage, going ever deeper into the causes of problems – although this may be very interesting, it is not always necessarily useful.

The most common shortcoming I experience with the managers I work with, however, is that they tend not to spend enough time on this stage. They rush into solutions without enough information or understanding, and without having helped the other person think through what is going wrong. Time spent at this stage asking questions about the causes of problems is rarely time wasted.

# Prioritize areas for learning

The analysis of problems is likely to throw up a number of potential issues which could be addressed at the action planning stage and probably more issues than can be usefully dealt with at any one time. If this is the case, it is necessary to prioritize them so that you focus on the issues which will be most useful and productive.

Ideally this decision should be made by the other person. Your role should be to help that person make the right decision. This involves three steps:

- Summarizing to clarify the analysis that you have arrived at. For example: 'There are several things we could address. The level of detail in your initial structure; the need to identify the key messages; the style of your writing; the extent to which you get absorbed in the content and forget the function of the report; the way you read your first draft; your need to write the perfect report.'

- Asking the other person to prioritize what should be addressed. For example: 'What do you think will be the most useful issue to address first in terms of your report-writing generally?' 'If we were to look at two of these things now, which are the ones that you need to focus on first?'

- Helping the other person to evaluate priorities: 'I agree that you need to read your first drafts in a more disciplined way, but do you think that is going to be the best place to start?' 'Do you think it might help if we made sure your first drafts were better structured, so that they did not need a lot of rewriting?'

In this way, you can help clarify the other person's immediate needs and identify the most valuable areas to be addressed. Skills activity 10.5 will help you to practise this.

## *SKILLS ACTIVITY 10.5: PRIORITIZING*

Using the practice opportunity you selected in Skills activity 10.1, prioritize the one or two areas the person needs to focus on next to improve performance and then plan how you will help the person to identify those priorities personally.

202 Managing people

# Develop an action plan

We are now at the end of the funnel. We have gathered a full and accurate picture, reinforced the positives, identified the problem areas, analyzed them, and prioritized one or two areas which will provide suitable next steps for the person's learning and development. *Now* is the time to think about solutions to the problems!

There are two parts to this last stage of the reviewing process. The first is to identify solutions; the second is to plan how they will be implemented. It is because of this second part that the stage is called 'developing an action plan'. The underlying principle is that learning should lead to action, because it is through action that the learning can be applied, evaluated and reinforced.

In both parts, identifying solutions and action planning, you have three choices about what behaviour to use. These are to do the following:

- **Propose** your own solutions for how the issue could be addressed. For example: 'I think you need to structure your reports in more detail, so that you have planned the content for each section in outline before you start writing.' 'Under each section heading in your structure, write down a summary of the key message that section needs to convey.'

- **Suggest** one or more options for the other person to evaluate. For example: 'Would it help if you defined the content for each section in more detail before you started writing?' 'How useful would it be if you wrote down a summary of the key message that section needs to convey alongside the section headings in your structure?'

- **Ask** the other person to put forward his or her own ideas for how the issue could be addressed. For example: 'How could you define the content for each section more clearly at the planning stage?' 'How could you keep the key messages you are trying to convey at the front of your mind as you write the first draft?'

Which behavioural option you choose will depend on the needs of the other person. The choice here is similar to choosing which coaching style to use – you will find further information about this choice in Chapter 6. In general, it is always better for other people to develop their own solutions and action plans. You should only suggest or propose if you feel that they are unlikely to come up with an appropriate solution on their own.

The review should finish with agreement about one or more

actions that the person will take in the near future to improve their performance. These actions should be:

- **Specific:** Not vague promises or intentions, but definite actions which will happen within a specified time.

- **Achievable:** Actions which the person will be able to carry out, even if they are difficult and challenging.

- **Soon:** Actions that will be carried out within two weeks of the review discussion wherever possible.

## *SKILLS ACTIVITY 10.6: ACTION PLANNING*

Using the practice opportunity you selected in Skills activity 10.1, identify the solutions and specific next steps that you want the other person to take to improve his or her performance and then plan how you will help the other person arrive at these solutions and decide how to implement them.

# Summary: managing content

In this chapter, we have looked at the principles, structures and skills involved in reviewing someone's performance or specific events and experiences. The structure and skills are summarized in Figure 10.1. This provides a simplified version of the reviewing process which you could use as a guide to help you plan and conduct review discussions. End this chapter by doing Skills activity 10.7 which asks you to practise reviewing skills.

## *SKILLS ACTIVITY 10.7: CONTENT*

Carry out the review that you have selected as the basis for the Skills activities in this chapter. They should have provided you with a plan for a review which will help the other person learn from his or her experience.

When you have carried out the review, use the six-stage structure detailed in this chapter to reflect on your performance as coach in the review discussion.

| Stage | Behaviour | Example |
|---|---|---|
| 1. Gather data | 'What' questions to seek detailed information. | • What did Jack actually say?<br>• What happened next? |
| 2. Consolidate strengths | Questions and feedback to identify and explore strengths | • I was pleased with the way you . . . why do you think it went so well? |
| 3. Identify weak points | Summarize and seek agreement | • So you find it difficult to be criticized and not react defensively, is that right? |
| 4. Analyze weak points | 'Why' questions to explore causes of problems etc. | • Why do you find it difficult?<br>• Why did you react . . . ? |
| 5. Prioritize | Summarize and seek priorities | • The areas we could focus on are . . . which would be most useful to you? |
| 6. Action plan | 'How' questions to seek solutions and specific actions | • How can you avoid such delays in the future?<br>• How can you put that into practice? |

**Figure 10.1**  Effective reviewing

# 11

# Commitment

In Chapter 10, we looked at the basic requirements for effectively handling interactions that involve the reviewing of activities and performance. The structure and skills covered in that chapter will be appropriate in most situations when the person you are helping is open to critically evaluating their performance and is committed to improving it. Although this will be true most of the time, it will not necessarily be true all of the time! There will be occasions when your people will resist your attempts to manage or improve their performance.

In this chapter, we shall focus on the strategies and skills required to overcome resistance and generate commitment in people so that they do what you want them to do. We will look at the following areas:

- The basis of resistance.
- Strategies for developing the need for change.
- The skills involved in developing need and commitment.

The strategies and skills covered in this chapter will help you to become more effective in any situation where you have to be persuasive – not just with people-management issues.

# The basis of resistance

Resistance to change is a complex process, which reflects the individual's personality as much as any rational considerations about the rights and wrongs of the change in question. However, at the root of this process there is usually a simple calculation, which goes as follows:

- What is this change going to cost me?
- How am I going to benefit from it?
- Do the costs outweigh the benefits?

For most people, this calculation will be their instinctive response to any demand you make of them which requires them to change the way they do things. Your attempts to persuade them and get their commitment to what you want are, in essence, attempts to influence the way they make that calculation. The two key components are:

- **Cost:** This might be financial cost, or time, effort, hassle, risk of failure, loss of status and so on.

- **Benefit:** This might be financial gain, savings in time and effort, improvements to working conditions, increased job satisfaction, greater opportunities to develop, greater recognition and so on.

If the perceived cost of change is greater than the perceived benefit, the change is likely to be resisted. I will give you an example from my own experience: I bought a new computer with an integrated software package over a year ago now. From the moment I bought it, I have intended to get some training to help me use the computer to its full potential. I have not done it. I have some idea what the benefits will be, I know I ought to do it. I have not done it. My perception of the cost involved has outweighed my perception of the benefit. For me, the major cost is not financial, it is:

- Finding the time to do it.
- Anxiety about being able to learn new skills.
- Concern that the training will not address my needs.
- Repeating the frustration that I have felt with the computer training I have received in the past.

Even though these costs are not considerable, they are enough to outweigh the benefits I think I will get. To understand why this is the case, we must break benefit down into its two component parts: value and need.

## Value and need

Our perception of the benefit of change is made up of two parts:

- The value we think the change will have for us in the future.
- The need we have to change what we are doing now.

These may sound similar but are quite different, and their difference is at the heart of effective persuasion. In my example, although I know that I am likely to learn how to get better value out of my computer if I do some training, I do not feel that I really *need* to use my computer better than I do at the moment. I get by. I know it is not perfect, I know it could be a lot better, but I am not dissatisfied enough with my present situation to try and change it. And *that* is why I do not do any training. Use Exercise 11.1 to think about a similar experience of your own.

## *EXERCISE 11.1*

> Spend a few minutes now reflecting on times when someone has tried to persuade you to change the way you do something. To what extent did your perception of the need to change differ from the other person's perception of value?

The mistake we often make when we are persuading people is to confuse need with value, and to assume that our perception of the value of change will be the same as their perception of the need to change. To understand the causes of someone's resistance, **we must first assess their perception of the *need* to change**.

## The development of need

Our need to change is based on how we feel about our present situation and our awareness of the problems we have in that situation. In my case, my dissatisfaction with the way I was using the computer grew as the range and amount of work I did on it increased. When all I did was word processing, and when I was not too busy, there was no problem. When I started using the graphics and spreadsheet packages, things got more difficult. And I found myself with less and less time to sort out any difficulties. I was having to work late on fiddly bits of artwork and was getting increasingly frustrated when things did not go right. I have got to the stage now where I feel I have to do something because the list of dissatisfactions below form a powerful basis of need. I am:

- Worried about whether I make back-up copies of my work regularly enough.
- Frustrated with the time it takes me to use the graphics software.
- Increasingly irritated when things happen that I do not understand.
- Not satisfied with the quality of artwork I am able to achieve.
- Doubtful that I am making best use of the spreadsheet to do my accounts.
- Concerned that I am using the computer efficiently enough to cope with the increased workload that I am generating.

This development of need over time is typical, as illustrated in Figure 11.1.

Our need to change usually starts as a small dissatisfaction with how things are in the present, or concern about what will happen in the future. We do not do anything at this stage, because the need is not big enough. If the dissatisfaction grows, so too does our need to change. If the dissatisfaction grows big enough, we will start to

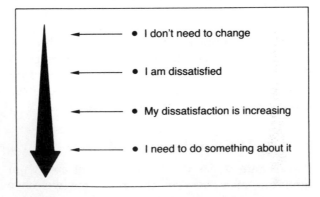

**Figure 11.1** Development of need

contemplate action. It is only now, when I feel that I *must* do something about my computer skills, that I will look seriously at the prospect of doing some training.

Although I now feel that I must do something, this does not necessarily mean that I will. I know what my problems are. I now need to think about what the **value** to me of doing some training will be. I need to be convinced that it will be worth my while to set aside time to do some training, as illustrated in Figure 11.2.

The following are some of the benefits that I could obtain:

- Peace of mind about having proper back-up for my hard disk.
- Less time spent fiddling around with graphics, which means
- More time to focus on the quality of the text, and
- Fewer late nights in front of the computer.
- Being less stressed and irritable when using the computer, and so
- Being more friendly to people who phone me up when I am using it!
- Better quality graphics on my proposals and materials.
- Invoices and accounts done more easily, with less scope for error.
- Increased ability to use new pieces of software in the future.
- More informed discussions with people I need to interface with.

When I think about the value in this way, my motivation to do something increases yet further. If I can achieve even some of that,

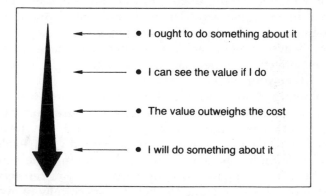

**Figure 11.2** The development of the awareness of value

then the pay-off will more than justify the cost involved. Use Exercise 11.2 to reflect on a similar experience of your own.

## *EXERCISE 11.2*

Spend a few minutes now reflecting on times when you have decided to change some aspect of your life (e.g. buy a new car, take more exercise, organize your work better). Think about the process that you went through to reach the decision to change, focusing on:

- The increase of your dissatisfaction with the present.
- Your growing awareness of the value of change.

# Strategies for developing need

I wish now that I had done some training six months ago. I wish that somebody had helped me then to anticipate the problems I was likely to experience in the future. I wish somebody had developed my awareness of the need to do some training so that I actually did it, rather than just thought about it. Left to its own devices, my need grew too slowly – partly because I did not have the knowledge or experience to anticipate the kind of problems I am experiencing now. I needed somebody to help me.

The trouble is, that if you know something about computers, you will know that I should have gone on some training and you will know why. But because something seems blindingly, obviously, unarguably right to us, this does not mean that the other person will see things in the same way! There is one central premise behind effective persuasion: **being right is not persuasive!**

In some ways, knowing about computers will make it harder for you to be effective in persuading me, because it increases the likelihood that your 'strategy' will be to tell me that I should do some training and to explain all the benefits that I will get from doing so. In other words, you would have focused on value, but you would not have addressed my need – and therefore would probably have failed to convince me. If you do not explore my needs, you can only talk about value in a vacuum – the benefits as *you* see them. If you know what my needs are, you can focus your description of value by relating the benefits specifically to my needs.

The focus on our solutions and the value we see in them is at the heart of what goes wrong in countless persuasions. We try to prove to the person that we are right – and whether we are right or wrong is immaterial. What is important is whether the person *needs* what we want them to do. You can tell me how computer training will improve the quality of my life. Rationally, I might even agree with you. But unless I am convinced that I need it, I ain't going to do it! Because we believe that all we have to be is right, we make the mistake of trying to develop people's perception of the *value* of the change when we should be focusing on developing the *need* for it.

## EXERCISE 11.3

Spend a few minutes now reflecting on times when you have tried to persuade someone to do something they were reluctant to do. To what extent did you try to convince them that you were right about the value of the change? To what extent did you try to develop their need to change?

In order to overcome resistance and generate commitment, we need to use a strategy that is based on the following four steps:

1. Develop the need for change.
2. Develop awareness of the value of change.
3. Develop ownership of the solution.
4. Develop solutions that minimize cost.

The sequence of these steps is important, and is based on two underlying principles:

- It is better to develop the need before you develop the solution. If people feel they need the solution, they are more likely to be positive when you engage them in developing it.
- It is better to increase the awareness of value before trying to reduce the perception of cost. If people feel there is value in changing, their perception of cost is likely to reduce. And people are more likely to enagage constructively on how to manage the cost if they feel that there is sufficient value.

We will look at each of the four steps in turn, and then go on to look at the specific skills required to carry them out.

# Develop the need for change

The first step is to develop other people's awareness of the need to change by focusing on their dissatisfactions with the present and their concerns about the future. These may be dissatisfactions and concerns that they already feel: for example, my frustration with the time it takes to me to do graphics. Or they may be ones that they *should* feel: for example, anxiety about what happens to the work I only have on hard disk if there is a power cut!

If you were trying to persuade me to get some training, you should first help me to understand the price I pay for the way I use the computer at the moment.

# Develop awareness of the value of change

Dissatisfaction alone will not be enough. There are a number of things I recognize as problems with my present way of working that I do not bother to address. Sometimes this inertia is because the dissatisfaction is not big enough, sometimes it is because the cost still outweighs the value. So the second step in the persuasion strategy is to develop other people's awareness of the value of change. Most of the value will be the resolution of the dissatisfactions and problems experienced in the present. But there are likely to be other values that they may not be aware of. It is likely that, if I improve in using the computer, there will be benefits that I cannot imagine at the moment.

If you were trying to persuade me to take some training, you would need to help me to recognize those benefits – in terms of how it could make my life easier.

# Develop ownership of the solution

Whenever possible, you should involve the people you are persuading in developing specific solutions for achieving what you want them to do. If you help me to decide how to go about developing my usage of the computer you will be increasing my commitment to the solution that is agreed, because I will feel:

- I have some power in the situation.
- You respect my ability to solve my own problems.
- I have some ownership of the eventual solution.
- My concerns have been taken into account.

If, on the other hand, you tell me that I must go on a training programme on computer skills, none of these things will happen. I may go on the programme, but because I have not been involved in identifying the solution, I am less likely to be committed – and so you run the risk of me wriggling out of going or refusing to learn anything from it if I do go.

If there is only one solution possible, it will be less easy to develop other people's ownership; but you can still involve them in deciding *how* the solution can best be implemented. For example, if, for some reason, you have to send me on a training programme, you can involve me in discussing how I can best make use of it, given that it is not my preferred way of learning. Are there things I can do before, during or after the programme which will make that solution more acceptable to me?

## Develop solutions that minimize cost

So far, we have addressed two of the three elements of resistance: need and value. The intention has been to develop an awareness of value that outweighs the perception of cost. But even when this is done successfully, the cost element does not go away and still needs to be handled.

It is best to address cost at the solution stage, partly because it will be balanced by the perception of value, and partly because you can deal with it at a practical level. If you clarify what the cost concerns are, you can develop a solution which will resolve as many of them as possible. For example, my computer training could be built around work that I have to do: this will resolve some of my concerns about the relevance of the training to my needs.

It is unlikely that you will be able to resolve all the costs in this way – there is usually a price to be paid for change! But by getting the concerns on to the table, and exploring ways of resolving them, you will be signalling your desire to help other people manage the costs, and this will have a positive impact on their commitment to what is finally agreed. Use Exercise 11.4 to apply this to your own experience.

## *EXERCISE 11.4*

Spend a few minutes now reflecting on an interaction you have had recently when you have tried to persuade someone to change an aspect of their performance. It should be an interaction which you feel you could have managed more effectively.

> Use the four-stage structure for developing need and generating commitment to help you identify the causes of difficulty you experienced in the interaction and to plan ways in which you could manage it more effectively if you were to tackle the issue again.

# Planning a persuasion

We usually become involved in persuasive interactions without any planning or preparation. Often this is because we did not anticipate that we would have to be persuasive. Sometimes is is because we did not spend enough time thinking it through beforehand. Either way, we usually pay the price. If you know that you are going to have to persuade people, here are some key questions you can ask yourself to help you plan how best to manage the interaction.

- **What will their perception of cost be?** If you can anticipate how they are likely to perceive the cost of what you want them to do, you will be able to anticipate how resistant they are likely to be (i.e. high cost = high resistance).

- **Is there more than one possible solution?** Check whether you are confusing solutions with outcomes (see Chapter 5). You will always be in a stronger position if you have a range of possible ways of achieving your desired outcome – this gives you much more room for manoeuvre.

- **What's in it for them?** Make a list of the benefits that they will gain from doing what you want them to do. Then put yourself in their shoes and think about how many of the benefits on your list they will perceive as valuable.

- **What needs does my outcome address?** Make a list of the problems, dissatisfactions or concerns that the other people have at the moment (whether they are aware of them or not) which would be addressed by your desired outcome. Some of these may be covered by your answers to the previous question. It is surprising, though, how focusing on needs can throw up different issues.

## SKILLS ACTIVITY 11.1: PERSUASION PLANNING

> If possible, identify a situation in the near future where you want to encourage someone to change an aspect of his or her performance. Alternatively, identify an instance in the recent past where you have had to persuade somebody on a performance issue.
>
> Use the questions above to help you plan how you are going to develop the person's need for change and generate commitment to your desired outcome.

The questions listed above will help you to identify:

- The level of resistance you are likely to encounter. The higher this is, the more careful you will have to be in planning an effective strategy.
- The level of flexibility you have. The greater this is, the more chance you will have of generating commitment when you develop solutions.
- The level of pay-off. The higher this is, the greater your chances of getting involvement in developing solutions.
- The level of need. The higher this is, the greater your chances of generating the motivation to change.

In short, the answers to these questions will tell you how easy your job is likely to be. For example, if resistance is high, and there is little pay-off, then it will be very difficult. It may be best to issue instructions about what you want, and then help the other person work out a way of complying. In such a scenario, trying to persuade through rational discussion is unlikely to prove productive.

---

# Skills

---

We have seen earlier in the book that when you are coaching, you need to choose which style of behaviour will best suit the requirements of the person you are helping. There are three coaching styles: directing, guiding and enabling.

When you are persuading someone, there is a similar choice about style. There are two basic styles:

- **Push:** This is the equivalent of directing: you tell the other person what you want done; you explain your reasons. You persuade through the power of your position or personality.

- **Pull:** This is the equivalent of enabling: you use questions to develop the other person's need for what you want and to evoke co-operation in identifying specific was of achieving it. You persuade by developing the person's need for change.

As with coaching, both styles can be effective. The key is to choose the right style for the situation you are facing. Use Exercise 11.5 to think about your own persuasion style.

## EXERCISE 11.5

Spend a few minutes now reflecting on the style of behaviour you tend to use when you are persuading people to do something. Do you tend to use a **push** style most of the time? Are there times when you will use a **pull** style?

Most people will instinctively choose a **push** style when they have to be persuasive. It is the most straightforward and quickest way. And most of the time it will be appropriate, because the level of resistance from the other person will not be great. The push style will be less effective, however, when you need to generate the other person's commitment to ensure that the change will be implemented.

If you need commitment, it is likely that the questioning style will be more effective. It is also the most appropriate style to use if you want to encourage and help people to review their performance critically, learn from their experiences, and take ownership of their own development. It is for these reasons that the questioning style of persuasion will be appropriate in most people-management interactions.

## Strategic questions

In the previous chapter, we established a six-stage structure for helping someone to review their performance, and looked at the

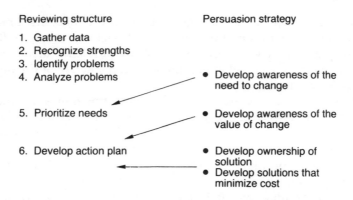

**Figure 11.3**  Persuasion strategy

kind of questions you need to ask at each stage. The reviewing structure will be effective when the people you are helping are not resistant to change. When they are, you need to insert the persuasion strategy into the basic reviewing structure, as illustrated in Figure 11.3.

Each step of the persuasion strategy requires you to ask specific kinds of question which are focused at influencing the perceptions and gaining the commitment of the other person. We will now explore the skills involved in the questioning style of persuasion, looking at each step of the strategy in turn.

## Developing the need for change

At this first step in the process, you need to ask questions which make other people focus on their dissatisfactions with the present or concerns about the future. For example: 'Are you **confident** that you are not wasting memory on the hard disk?' 'Are you **worried** about what would happen to the work on your hard disk if there was a power cut?' 'How **irritated** do you get with the time it takes you to do graphics work on the computer?' 'How **satisfied** are you with the way you use the spreadsheet functions on your book-keeping and invoicing?'

The bold words in each example give these questions their strategic value. It is these words that make the questions probe directly for dissatisfaction. In this instance, they are forcing me to review the problems that I am having with the computer, and raising my awareness of problems that I had not previously considered.

These questions will not automatically uncover concerns: I may be totally satisfied with how I use the spreadsheet, for example. But, if they help me to recognize the extent of my problems, anxieties and frustrations, they will be helping me to become aware of the need to change how I do things at the moment.

Although the key words have the same function – to uncover needs – the examples show that this can be done in different ways:

- In the questions about memory and the spreadsheet, the key words were positive: 'confident', 'satisfied' – to which you could add: pleased, happy, secure, relaxed, comfortable, find it easy, have no trouble, etc. If I answer 'no' to these questions, I am stating a need.

- In the questions about back-up copies and graphics, the key words were negative: 'worried', 'irritated' – to which you could add: concerned, hassled, afraid, anxious, dissatisfied, unhappy, find it difficult, struggle, take too long, etc. If I answer 'yes' to these questions, I am stating a need.

Questions like these help someone to become aware that the present is not perfect. By using them, you can uncover a number of needs which, when put together, generate the motivation to take action. But you may not have developed the need enough. I might now recognize that I am not as happy as I thought I was, but I am not yet convinced that I need to do something about it.

If this is the case, you have to develop my need further, by getting me to see the **consequences** of the problems I have acknowledged. No problem exists in a vacuum – it causes other problems, or potential problems, which can be exposed by asking questions like this: 'What would the **consequences** be for you if you lost everything on your hard disk?' 'Are you dissatisfied with the final appearance of your work **as a result** of your difficulty with the graphics package?' 'Does your irritation **spill over** into other aspects of your work?' 'How much time do you waste **because** of the way you use the spreadsheet at the moment?'

Again, the bold words in each example give these questions their strategic value. They can be very persuasive, as they force people to think more deeply and more critically about their current situation. They can uncover issues and problems that people were not aware of or were trying to ignore, and by doing so, develop the need for change to the point where people are ready to consider action. Skills activity 11.2 will help you practise this.

## *SKILLS ACTIVITY 11.2: NEED QUESTIONS*

> Using the situation you identified in Skills activity 11.1, plan the questions you could ask to develop the person's awareness of the need to change. These questions should probe for concerns and dissatisfactions that the other person has or should have with the way he or she does things at the moment.

## Developing awareness of the value of change

It is tempting, when you feel you have developed the need for change sufficiently, to start to develop the solutions. In some cases, it may be OK to do so. If you had asked me the four questions about my relationship with my computer on the previous page, I would probably have said that it was a fair cop, I'd come quietly. But even in cases like that, it is best to spend time developing the awareness of the value of change before discussing how the change can best be achieved, for two reasons:

- Even though the need is strong, this does not mean that the perceived value of change will outweigh the perception of cost.
- By exploring the value, you can acquire a more specific understanding of the kind of solution that is required.

In order to do this, you need to ask questions which persuade the other person to focus on what they will gain from changing. For example: 'Would you feel **more secure** if you knew you had back-up copies for all your work?' 'In what ways would having a better system for back-up copies **benefit** you with the work you'll be doing over the next year?' 'Do you think you're going to **need** more sophisticated graphics given the work that you've got coming up?' 'How much time do you think you could **save** in a week if you were more skilled using the graphics program?' 'Which has more **value** for you in the short term, getting better at using graphics or the spreadsheet?'

It is the bold words that give these questions their strategic value. They are helping me to recognize the benefits of improving my use of the computer, and also helping me to prioritize my needs by looking at the relative values of tackling different aspects of the problem. They are increasing the value of change so that it becomes bigger than the costs involved. Use Skills activity 11.3 to practise phrasing such questions.

## *SKILLS ACTIVITY 11.3: VALUE QUESTIONS*

Using the situation you identified in Skills activity 11.1, plan the questions you could ask to develop the person's awareness of the value of change. These questions should help the person see how life will be improved if the problems already identified through the need questions are addressed.

# Developing ownership of the solution

When people are fully aware of the need for and the value of change, they should be in a positive frame of mind for exploring possible solutions. It is tempting at this stage to present them with your solution, telling them what you want them to do or what you think they should do. But awareness of need and value alone will not necessarily develop commitment. For this to happen, other people need to feel some ownership over what is going to happen to them. To generate feelings of ownership, you need to involve other people in the process of developing the solution.

In the previous chapter, we identified three ways of generating solutions at the action planning stage of the reviewing structure. When you are using a questioning style to gain commitment, the best option is to ask them to propose ideas themselves, using questions like: 'What would be the best way of helping you improve your use of the graphics software?' 'How do you want to tackle the different issues we've identified?' 'What will be the best way of reviewing what you store on floppy disk?' 'How would you like the training to be organized?'

Questions like these give total responsibility to other people to generate their own solutions. They give them the opportunity to consider their preferred options, which will probably resolve some of the costs they associate with the change.

If, however, you feel that they will not be able to come up with ideas themselves, the next best option is to suggest ideas for them to evaluate, using questions like: 'Would it be best if someone spent a day with you in your office and gave you feedback on how you used the computer?' 'How would you feel about going on a training programme on using the spreadsheet?' 'Would it be useful if you came and watched me doing some graphics work for half a day, so that you could see the short cuts I use?'

Questions like these give partial responsibility to other people. They will be appropriate if you feel that they are unlikely to come up with their own ideas. They give them the opportunity to evaluate your preferred options and reject them if they do not feel suitable. If they do reject your ideas, the questions will have stimulated them to consider alternatives.

Either of these options are effective ways of generating feelings of ownership and thus commitment. They each, however, carry a certain risk: the other person may come up with proposals that you do not like, or which are not acceptable to you. If this happens, you need to find a way of responding to their proposals which does not take away their feeling of ownership. There are two approaches, depending on the level of acceptability of their proposal.

For the totally unacceptable proposal, state your concern with the proposal and ask the person concerned to explore alternatives which will be more acceptable to both parties. For example: 'If I get someone to sort out your back-up copies for you, you're not going to learn to do it for yourself. What other options would you feel comfortable with?' For the partially unacceptable proposal, agree with the parts of the proposal you like, and try to modify the parts that you do not like to make them more acceptable. For example, 'I'm happy to show you how I use my spreadsheet, but I'm not sure that just showing you will be enough. Why don't you copy your accounts on to a floppy disk and bring them with you so that we can work on those together as well.'

Both these ways of responding leave the other person with some ownership of the final solution. Some ownership is better than no ownership if you need to generate commitment to ensure that they carry out the actions that are agreed. Practise generating solutions in Skills activity 11.4.

## SKILLS ACTIVITY 11.4: GENERATING SOLUTIONS

Using the situation you identified in Skills activity 11.1, plan how best to develop the other person's ownership of and commitment to solutions which achieve the change you desire. Anticipate the kind of proposals the other person is likely to make and plan how to handle them if you feel they are inappropriate.

## Developing solutions that minimize cost

There have been several times in my life when I have assumed that the person I am persuading is committed to the solution that we have agreed, only to find out that it has not been implemented because the person concerned had second thoughts after our meeting. These are the concerns the person has about the cost of change, and they can reassert themselves with nagging insistency when the person has a few quiet moments to think about it. So the final stage in the process is to try to prevent these second thoughts by dealing with the elements of cost within the solution you develop. This involves two steps:

- Uncovering the person's concern with the change that is being discussed, and the barriers that are likely to get in the way of the change being implemented successfully. For example: 'How easy is it going to be for you to free up the time to spend with me on the computer?' 'What have your experiences of computer training been like in the past? Are you thinking that it's all going to be too complicated for you to remember?'

- Adding to the solution wherever possible so that it reduces the costs involved. For example, 'If time is going to be a problem, why don't you bring a piece of work that you need to do with you, and I can show how I would use the graphics software to do it? That would probably save you time as well as developing your capability.'

Now use Skills activity 11.5 to practise this yourself.

## *SKILLS ACTIVITY 11.5: HANDLING COST*

Using the situation you identified in Skills activity 11.1, plan how you can uncover the person's concerns about the cost of the change you want to make. Then see if there are ways you can modify the solutions you have identified which will reduce the impact of these cost concerns.

# Summary: generating commitment

In this chapter, we have looked at the strategy and skills involved in overcoming resistance and generating commitment to change. These are summarized in Figure 11.4. This provides a simplified version of the persuasion process which you could use as a guide to help you to plan and conduct such interactions.

| Stage | Behaviour | Example |
|---|---|---|
| 1. Develop awareness of need | 'Need' questions to uncover and build on dissatisfactions with the present and concerns about the future | • Do you waste time making mistakes using the graphics package?<br>• Are you disappointed by the quality of your finished product? |
| 2. Develop awareness of value | 'Value' questions to explore the benefits of change and specify the kind of solution required. | • How else would you use graphics if you were more confident?<br>• Why would it be useful if your proposals were done with graphics? |
| 3. Develop ownership of solution | Seek proposals from the other person or suggest options for them to evaluate | • How would you like to improve your use of the graphics package?<br>• Would it be a good idea to use an old proposal to develop a template without any time pressure? |
| 4. Develop solutions to reduce cost | 'Cost' questions to uncover concerns and develop the solution to overcome them. | • Are you worried that I'll dazzle you with science?<br>• Would it be better if we used two computers so you had hands on experience of what I am doing? |

**Figure 11.4** Generating commitment to change

## SKILLS ACTIVITY 11.6: COMMITMENT

Carry out the persuasive interaction that you have selected as the basis for the skills activities in this chapter. They should have provided you with a plan that will help you to overcome the person's resistance and generate their commitment to change.

The skills that we have focused on in this chapter are not easy to apply and you should not expect to put them into action immediately. If you are not used to strategic questioning, you will probably find Skills activity 11.6 difficult. If this is the case, it will be better for you to focus on one stage of the process at a time: asking need questions, for example, or uncovering concerns. Select the practice step that will be most useful for you and that you will be able to achieve relatively easily.

# 12

# Confrontation

If you manage people, there will inevitably be times when you have to confront them with your negative feelings. This may be because they are not working to the standard you expect, or because they are behaving inappropriately, or because of tensions in your relationship with them. Whatever the reason, you need to make sure they understand that what they are doing is unacceptable.

Most managers feel uncomfortable at the prospect of confronting someone about such issues. This is understandable: it is difficult to do well, and you can make things worse if you do it badly. For roughly half of the managers that I have trained in people management over the last six years, the skill area that they have most wanted to develop is that of confronting difficult issues and giving critical feedback. This is the aspect of their people-management work which they find most difficult, feel least able to do well and which they find the most stressful.

There are two parts to the problem. Some managers tend to avoid confrontation and want to develop the confidence to tackle people about poor performance issues. Others feel that, when they do confront people, they do not do it very well – they want to develop the skills of effective confrontation. In this chapter we will look at both these issues: first by exploring some of the principles involved in deciding whether to confront someone; second, by examining some of the skills involved in delivering negative messages effectively. Do Exercise 12.1 before you read on.

*EXERCISE 12.1*

Spend a few minutes now reflecting on your own confidence and ability to confront difficult issues with people. Do you feel that you do confront issues when they arise, or do you tend to avoid them if you can? When you do confront them, do you feel you do it effectively or not?

Before we go on, I want to clarify the distinction I am making here between confrontation and conflict. I am using confrontation to describe the process of constructively tackling a difficult issue with someone. This is different from conflict. Conflict is what is likely to happen if confrontation is either avoided or badly handled. We will start by looking at the issue of avoidance, and the risks involved in failing to confront difficult issues.

# The avoidance cycle

I have developed a model, called the avoidance cycle, which helps people to recognize the dynamics of confrontation and conflict. Figure 12.1 illustrates the key stages of the cycle, which are explained in detail below. The avoidance cycle illustrates how conflict situations can develop when people avoid confronting difficult issues. And avoidance is very common. What typically happens is as follows:

1.  **There is a problem.** It is inevitable in all relationships that, sooner or later, someone will do something that irritates you. This might be minor: the person you share an office with is noisy. Or it may be more serious: someone turns up late for a meeting, misses a deadline, makes a mistake, ignores your instructions; a colleague is confused, or insensitive, or ungenerous, or negative, or aggressive. From the point that this happens for the first time, a new dynamic enters the relationship, and you have to decide whether to address it: 'should I say something?'

2.  **You do not address it.** You decide not to say anything. There may be several reasons why you do not, but, typically, it will feel too risky. So the dynamic remains unaddressed. If the issue does not arise again, the matter will end here – perhaps positive

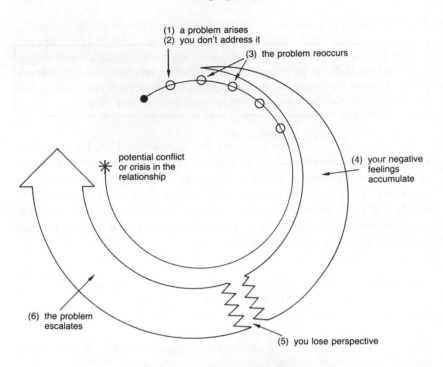

**Figure 12.1**   The avoidance cycle

experiences in the relationship will soon outweigh this negative one, and the problem will be forgotten.

3. **The problem does not go away.** The person does it again, or something similar. It becomes apparent that it is part of who they are and the way they operate – or the way that they react to you. It is no isolated incident: they are noisy, disorganized, careless; they do not evaluate how to behave very well; you make them nervous. You become aware that the issue will be a feature of your relationship.

4. **Your negative feelings accumulate.** The size of the problem does not change. It is not that they become more noisy, disorganized or careless. What changes is the size of your feelings about the problem. Your negative feelings accumulate. The third time it happens, for example, you are more irritated by it than you were the first time. The more it happens the worse it gets.

5. **You lose perspective.** As your negative feelings accumulate, your ability to keep what is happening in perspective reduces, to the point where you lose perspective completely. Your responses become irrational. You start to use words like 'always' and 'never' to describe the other person's behaviour, and feel negative about everything your colleague does or says, regardless of merit. You may develop a persecution complex, believing the other person is deliberately trying to get at you.

6. **The problem escalates.** Once you have lost perspective, your ability to evaluate and control your own behaviour is greatly reduced. Your reactions to the person and his or her behaviour become more extreme and this makes the situation worse, increasing the tension between you, provoking conflict and often leading to some kind of crisis in the relationship. Typically, you will not be able to contain your feelings any more: you explode, overreacting to something which, in itself, is quite trivial. The other person is hurt and bewildered by the strength of your reaction. This can lead to conflict or some kind of crisis in the relationship.

Use Exercise 12.2 to apply the avoidance cycle to your own experience.

## EXERCISE 12.2

> Spend a few minutes now reflecting on whether there are situations at the moment where you are 'in' the avoidance cycle, i.e. issues which you are failing to confront and about which your negative feelings are accumulating.

The avoidance cycle is a remarkably common phenomenon. I have met few people who do not have a current example of a difficult issue that they are avoiding or a situation that is likely to deteriorate unless they say something soon.

## Facing things early

The key message of the avoidance cycle is that it is best to confront most difficult issues as early as possible. If you do not face the problem before your negative feelings accumulate, you are unlikely to be able to handle the confrontation effectively. Your feelings will get in the way, distorting your judgment and preventing you from communicating clearly – as anybody who has parented adolescent children, and disintegrated into an inarticulate heap on the floor, will know only too well!

There will be some situations, with some people, when we do face things quickly, sometimes immediately. We let the other person know how we are feeling and the problem is resolved. But it is likely that we will only feel safe to face things in this way with a few people. Generally, we say nothing, hoping the problem will go away, because saying something feels like too big a risk. This might be the risk of any of the following:

- Appearing oversensitive and vulnerable.
- Appearing overcritical and negative.
- Communicating badly and being misunderstood.
- Making the other person feel bad.
- Provoking a defensive and hurtful response.
- Arousing a negative response which does not resolve the problem.
- Causing a conflict that will make the situation worse.

All of these outcomes are possible. But they are less probable than you think. When we do not want to do something, we tend to create an exaggerated picture of the risks involved which justifies our inaction. I constantly work myself into a state about saying something to somebody who, when I do, responds so reasonably and positively that I am left wondering what all the fuss was about! In most cases, the *actual* risk will be much less than your *perception* of the risk.

The thing to remember is that the risk of *not* confronting the issue will almost always outweigh the risk of confronting it: firstly, because the problem is unlikely to go away of its own accord; secondly, because the longer you leave it, the harder it gets to say anything. This is not just because of the accumulation of negative feelings, but also because, as we lose perspective, we come to believe that the person will respond negatively if we say anything; in other words, our perception of the risk increases the longer we leave it. The key to confronting difficult issues is to face the problem as early as possible, when the risk involved is relatively small and your ability to manage it is relatively high.

# Monitoring your feelings

Although the message of the avoidance cycle is straightforward, putting it into practice is more difficult. It might be easier to confront issues early in the cycle, but that does not mean that it is easy. The first step is to monitor your feelings so that you are aware of the point when your negative feelings start to accumulate.

One of the ways that we subconsciously deal with the risk of confronting a difficult issue is to suppress our awareness of the problem. We will tell ourselves that it is not that important, or pretend that it is not happening. But the accumulation of negative feelings is a subconscious process, and it will not be fooled by these conscious attempts at self-deception. If we suppress our early awareness of difficulties, our negative feelings will accumulate before we can do anything about them. We will get to the point where we are amazed by the strength of our feelings.

Here are some steps you can take that will help you to monitor your feelings:

- When somebody does something that upsets you in some way, do not dismiss it: register that it happened and register how you responded.
- If it was sufficiently upsetting, face the issue as soon as you feel you are in a calm enough place to communicate effectively.
- If it was not too serious, wait and see if it happens again. If it does, monitor your response. We can usually sense whether our negative feelings are likely to accumulate. If that is the case, plan how best to confront the issue as soon as possible. We will be looking at how to do this later in this chapter; meanwhile do Exercise 12.3 to think about what you do with your feelings in difficult situations.

## *EXERCISE 12.3*

Spend a few minutes now reflecting on how you deal with your feelings when somebody does something that irritates or upsets you. Do you try to suppress them and hope the problem will go away? Or do you acknowledge the strength of the feeling and recognize that a potential problem is developing?

We all have emotional 'triggers', which are part of our psychology and emotional history. Particular things will upset us more than others, pulling these triggers and detonating emotional depth charges which reverberate dangerously and provoke extreme reactions. We tend to know when one of these depth charges is detonated because we can feel the subconscious rumblings of the explosion! Trust your gut feeling. However plausible your rational, conscious self is at persuading you that you are being silly – the feelings are there, and they will not go away.

# Facing things effectively

Having established that facing things early is usually likely to be the best strategy, it is now time to look at how to do this effectively. There are five elements involved in this:

- Clarifying your purpose.
- Defining the problem.
- Giving effective feedback.
- Making appropriate demands.
- Understanding resistance.

## Clarifying your purpose

One of the prerequisites of an effective interaction is that you are clear about your purpose. This is especially so when you are confronting difficult issues – if you are not clear about what you hope to achieve, it can be hard to extricate yourself from an increasingly entangled discussion.

In such situations, clarifying your purpose is complicated by the workings of the avoidance cycle. As your negative feelings accumulate, your purpose shifts from wanting to resolve the problem to wanting to blame and punish. You confront people because you want to prove their guilt, to show the problems that have been caused, to make them feel bad about giving you such grief. This is one of the reasons why it is so much harder to confront things effectively late on in the cycle: you want to get your own back!

So the first step in facing an issue effectively is to check out what you are hoping to achieve. Do you genuinely want to resolve the problem? Or do you want to 'punish' the other person? It is important that you are honest with yourself here. If your objective actually is to punish, then confrontation will probably lead to conflict. Few people enjoy being punished and the other person is likely to react defensively, responding emotionally rather than rationally. Resolution will be much harder to achieve.

If you do have a desire to punish, you need to recognize that the strength of your feelings will affect your ability to manage the interaction effectively. It is unlikely that you will be able to put these feelings to one side. It will be better for you not to confront the person until you have discharged some of the strength of your emotion – by talking it through with friends, for example. As much as possible, you should confront someone with the intention of reaching a positive outcome. Skills activity 12.1 asks you to identify an issue which you can use as a practise opportunity.

## *SKILLS ACTIVITY 12.1: CLARIFYING YOUR PURPOSE*

> If possible, identify a situation in the near future where you want to confront someone about an aspect of performance or behaviour which is causing you difficulty.
>
> Consider how far round the avoidance cycle you are with this issue, and the extent to which your purpose in having a confrontation is to do with punishment or resolution.

## Defining the problem

When other people irritate or upset us, we tend to think that *they* are the problem. *They* are doing something to us which we do not like. *They* are in the wrong. As you go further round the avoidance cycle, this definition of the problem becomes more entrenched and extreme – hence the desire to blame and punish the other person.

If you want to resolve the situation, it will help if you work from a different definition of the problem. Figure 12.2 illustrates that the issue is not just them and their behaviour. It is also you, and your reaction to the other person's behaviour. The problem is not one or other of you, it is the dynamic between you.

It can be difficult to accept this definition of the problem. It helps if you check out whether other people share your reaction to the issue. I remember once coming away from a meeting with a client

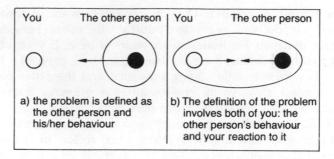

**Figure 12.2**   Defining the problem

seething about the way she had behaved, and was astonished to find out that my colleague had not seen it in the same way at all. His experience of the meeting was entirely different, and he had not been able to understand why I was getting so irritated. Even if he had felt the same as me, this would not have entitled me to define her as the problem. The real issue was as much about my response as it was about her behaviour. I struggled to accept this, but I had to if I was going to be able to handle the situation better at the next meeting. Use Skills activity 12.2 to apply this model.

## *SKILLS ACTIVITY 12.2: DEFINING THE PROBLEM*

Using the situation you identified in Skills activity 12.1, consider your definition of the problem. Do you define the problem as being *the other person*, or as being a combination of his/her behaviour and your response to it?

## Giving effective feedback

The way we define the problem affects how we confront the other person – it literally affects the words that we use. This can be seen by looking at the three ways in which we tend to communicate our negativity: criticism, feedback and advice.

### Criticism

When we do not like what other people do, we are essentially being critical of them and their behaviour. So when we say something, we tend to use criticism, saying in effect: 'you shouldn't do that.' These might not be the exact words, but the underlying message that will be received by the other person is the same: 'you shouldn't whistle when I'm on the phone.' 'you shouldn't turn up late for meetings.' 'you shouldn't make so many mistakes.' 'you shouldn't be so insensitive.'

The key word in these sentences, which conditions the underlying message that you are sending, is 'you'. It is this 'you' that tells the other people that you are defining *them* as the problem. And because this is the message they are receiving, it increases the likelihood that they will react defensively, either by denying the problem or attacking you back.

### Advice

Because we recognize that people do not like being criticized, we will often try to express our negativity more positively, by phrasing it as a suggestion for how other people could improve their behaviour or performance. Instead of criticism, we give advice, saying in effect: 'you should do this.' These may not be the exact words, but the underlying message that will be received by the other person is the same: 'you should be quieter when I'm on the phone.' 'you should make sure you turn up for meetings on time.' 'you should take more care over what you're doing.' 'you should listen more to what other people are saying.'

Again, the key word in these sentences, which conditions the underlying message that you are sending, is 'you'. It is this 'you' that tells the other person that you are defining them as the problem. And because this is the message, advice often has the same effect as criticism. It is worth remembering this maxim: **unwanted advice is heard as criticism**.

## EXERCISE 12.4

Spend a few minutes now reflecting on times when someone has given you a piece of unwanted advice. How did you respond? Did the advice sound like criticism to you? Reflect also on times when you have given people advice that they have not asked for – have they sometimes reacted to this as if you were being critical?

### Feedback

The alternative to criticism and advice is feedback. In this chapter, feedback is being given a more specific meaning than at other times in this book. When we use feedback, as opposed to criticism or advice, we are letting the other person know the impact they have on us, saying, in effect: 'we have a problem.' These might not be the exact words, but the underlying message that will be received by the other person is the same: 'I found it hard to hear what Jill was saying when you were whistling while I was talking to her on the phone.' 'I was irritated with you for turning up late for the meeting yesterday.' 'I get frustrated when you don't check your work carefully.' 'I'm upset that you don't seem to be interested in what I've got to say.' In these sentences, the key word which conditions the underlying message that you are sending is 'I'. It is this 'I' that tells the other person that you are defining the problem as a joint one, as something that happens between you. And because this is the message the other person is receiving, because the focus is shared between you, it increases the likelihood of a positive, rather than a defensive reaction.

There is another reason why feedback tends to be more effective than criticism and advice. By giving feedback, you are giving other people some valuable information: the way their behaviour affects you. One of the things that we cannot know about ourselves is the impact we have on others. We can imagine how people feel about us, but that can only be a projection of how we feel about ourselves. If you do not tell somebody that their behaviour upsets you, you are denying them the opportunity to improve the situation.

One of the features of the avoidance cycle is that you start to believe that the other people know how their behaviour affects you, because you think they are doing it deliberately to upset you. But in most cases they will not have a clue that you are responding in that way, and they will probably be grateful if you let them know. That is why the other key words in the examples of feedback above are the ones that describe impact: 'hard', 'irritated', 'frustrated', 'upset'. This is the same behaviour that we explored in the section on encouraging openness in Chapter 8, and the same principle applies. When you are confronting somebody, you want them to react as openly as possible, and the way to signal this is to be open yourself.

When people hear how you feel when they do something, they cannot argue with this: they cannot deny that you feel irritated or upset. They may feel that you should not respond to them in that way, but they have to accept that that *is* your response. And unless they have no interest in having a positive relationship with you, they will have to take your feelings into account.

There are three principles that you should bear in mind when you use feedback to confront difficult issues. These are:

- **Make it specific:** Deal with events rather than personalities, and specifics rather than generalities. For example: give feedback about how you find him disruptive when you make phone calls rather than about how noisy he is generally.

- **Make it small:** Deal with one event rather than several, and do not refer to the backlog of irritation that may have accumulated. For example: refer to one phone call when he was particularly disruptive (rather than 'every time I make a call you . . .!').

- **Make it recent:** Deal with a recent event which the other person will be able to remember clearly – if it was longer than two weeks ago, you should not refer to it unless it was a vivid experience. For example: refer to the last time he was disruptive when you were making a phone call.

By focusing your feedback in these three ways, you will make it easier for the other person to receive and therefore will make it easier to move towards resolution. Giving feedback effectively becomes much harder as you move through the avoidance cycle. As your objective moves towards punishment and blame, you will want to attack the other person's personality rather than behaviour and are more likely to come out with a stockpile of fermented generalities which will be too much for the other person to handle. Skills activity 12.3 asks you to practise giving feedback.

## *SKILLS ACTIVITY 12.3: GIVING FEEDBACK*

Using the situation you identified in Skills activity 12.1, write down the feedback you could give the other person which would help them to understand the impact of their behaviour on you. Remember to make your feedback:

- Specific.
- Small.
- Recent.

## Making appropriate demands

Giving feedback is the first step in effectively confronting difficult issues. If you plan carefully what you are going to say, this will with luck be the basis for a constructive exchange about the problem which leads naturally to a satisfactory resolution. Sometimes, however, things are not so straightforward, and the resolution does not emerge naturally out of the discussion. If this is the case, a further step is required, which is to make one or more **demands** which will improve the situation.

It helps if you identify the demands that you could make of the other person before you confront them. This is a useful way of checking out what your real purpose is: if the demands you want to make are unrealistic, this will be a tip-off that you are more interested in punishment than resolution. As we go through the avoidance cycle, and our perception of the size of the problem grows, so too does our perception of the size of the required solution. One way of taking ourselves back up the cycle is to focus on identifying small demands we can make that will improve the situation a little.

As with feedback, there are three principles to bear in mind when making effective demands. They should be:

- **Achievable:** The demand must be realistic, i.e. relatively easy for the other person to meet. It should provide a step in the right direction – not necessarily the total solution. The demand should generate a positive momentum in the relationship.

- **Specific:** The demand must be for a specific action or behaviour. Asking for reassurances that it will not happen again, for example, is not specific enough. Wherever possible, ask the other person to *do* something rather than not do something.

- **Soon:** The demand must be for something to be done soon, preferably specifying the time, although this is not always possible.

Here are some examples of effective demands: 'I've got a load of calls to make tomorrow. If I let you know before I start, could you be quiet while I am making them?' 'I'm going to be at the QIT meeting next week. Could you make sure you are there for the beginning of it?' 'The next time you give me a report to read, can you make sure you've checked it through yourself first?' 'When we have the budget meeting on the 18th, will you ask me for my opinion so that you involve me in the discussion?'

Skills activity 12.4 asks you to practise making demands.

## *SKILLS ACTIVITY 12.4: MAKING DEMANDS*

Using the situation you identified in Skills activity 12.1, write down the demands you could make of the other person which would create a positive momentum and provide steps towards resolving the problem. Remember to make your demands:

- Achievable.
- Specific.
- Soon.

## Understanding resistance

In most cases, giving feedback and making demands will enable you to manage the confrontation effectively. The other person will usually be happy to discuss the issue and find ways of resolving it. There may be times, however, when your attempts to address the problem are met with resistance of some kind: other people may refuse to discuss the issue or accept that there is a problem, or may try to retaliate by complaining about aspects of your behaviour; they may defend themselves by disagreeing with your perceptions of them or by justifying their behaviour.

When this happens, the interaction becomes much more difficult to manage. It is easy to get drawn into a confusing, unproductive and possibly destructive discussion which leaves you feeling worse than you did before. The core of the difficulty is that the other person is operating from a base of emotional resistance and so any attempt to deal with the situation rationally is doomed to failure. A useful tenet that will hold you in good stead is: **do not use rational argument to tackle emotional resistance!**

If you remember this, it could save you a lot of wasted breath and frustration in the future. The trouble is, it can be hard to tell the difference between rational and emotional resistance. Case study 12.1 is an example from my own experience which I hope will illustrate what I mean by emotional resistance and also show how hard it can be to identify it.

## CASE STUDY 12.1

I went with a client to discuss the implementation of a training project with the personnel director of one of his European sites. This was a site where traditionally there is a degree of hostility to head office. As we discussed the issues the personnel director continually threw in objections and counterproposals. At first, I took these at face value – they seemed quite rational suggestions, although they would be disruptive if we were to accommodate them. I spent some time trying to understand and modify his proposals to see if we could integrate them into our current plan. He resisted every attempt I made, disagreeing and suggesting even more divergent options. It became clear to me that the man was not coming from a rational base – and was not really interested in coming up with a solution that met all our needs. The meeting and the issue provided an arena for him to act out his emotional resistance to anything coming from head office. We could carry on until we were blue in the face and we would get nowhere.

## EXERCISE 12.5

Spend a few minutes now reflecting on the difference between rational and emotional resistance.

- First, think about a time when you were resisting somebody. To what extent was this resistance emotional? And to what extent did you cover this up with bogus rationality?
- Second, think about a time when you have tried to deal rationally with someone whose resistance was mainly emotional? Were you effective, or did your attempts 'feed' their resistance and make matters worse?

It is easy to fall into the trap of trying to overcome emotional resistance with facts and carefully constructed logic. It will get you nowhere. It will not touch the real causes of the resistance and can feed the other person with ammunition to use against you, tying you up in knots, confusing the issue, eroding your goodwill.

Emotional resistance is hard to spot because it often masquerades as rational argument. In my example, the man was not *behaving* emotionally, and what he was saying *seemed* reasonable. The tip-off was the way he resisted any attempt to come up with a solution. If you can recognize that you are dealing with emotional resistance and accept that the other person is not in a place to discuss the issue rationally, you can stop yourself from getting locked into a quick

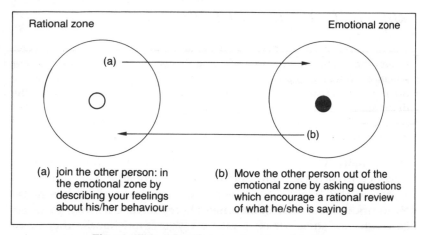

**Figure 12.3** Handling emotional resistance

and vicious version of the avoidance cycle – the interactive equivalent of a tumble dryer!

Identifying what kind of resistance you are dealing with will also help you to decide how to behave. The problem with using rational argument to address emotional resistance is that you are operating in different 'zones' and this is preventing you from making real contact. The principle of handling such situations is to try to get both of you in the same zone. There are two options here, as illustrated in Figure 12.3.

The first is to join the other person in the emotional zone, giving feedback, in the specific way described earlier in this chapter, to confront the issue of resistance. For example: 'I'm becoming concerned that we don't seem to be getting anywhere. It makes me wonder whether there is something beneath the surface we need to address.' 'I'm finding this frustrating because you don't seem interested in my attempts to come up with a solution which meets all our needs.' By describing your feelings, you are redirecting the conversation so that it addresses the emotional undercurrents rather than the surface issues.

The second is to try to move the other person into the rational zone by using questions to explore and expose the nature of the resistance. For example: 'Why is it so important for you to be the first site to receive the training?' 'Is the timescale we are suggesting going to cause significant problems on your site?' In both cases, the strategy is to uncover the underlying causes of resistance so that they can be at least acknowledged as an influence, even if they cannot be resolved.

## *SKILLS ACTIVITY 12.5: UNDERSTANDING RESISTANCE*

> Using the situation you identified in Skills activity 12.5, or another situation if that is more appropriate, reflect on the likely basis of the other person's resistance and identify ways in which you can manage the discussion so that you are both operating in the same zone.

Skills activity 12.5 is extremely difficult. Handling emotional resistance involves a high level of skill which cannot be adequately covered in this book. I hope, however, that the activity has helped you to understand why some interactions become so awkward, and has given you some ideas about how you could handle them more effectively. If it is any consolation, I wish I had used the examples above in the meeting with the personnel director, rather than realizing that they are what I should have said two hours later in the car on the way home!

## Summary: handling confrontation

In this chapter, we have looked at the some of the principles, strategies and skills involved in confronting difficult issues and people. The main messages can be summarized in the following five points:

- **Face the problem early.** The longer you leave it, the harder it will be to confront the problem effectively. The avoidance cycle will ensure that you lose perspective and, with it, the ability to evaluate how best to handle the situation.

- **Clarify your purpose.** Before you confront the person, make sure that your purpose is directed at resolution rather than punishment. Be honest! If you want to punish, the situation is more likely to escalate into a crisis of some kind.

- **Give feedback.** Give feedback rather than criticism or advice. This shows that you define the problem as a shared one and that you want to work towards resolution rather than blame. It also lets the other person know how you are affected – and this is valuable information (even if the other person does not seem overly appreciative at the time!).

- **Make realistic demands.** In order to move towards resolution, make demands of the person that, if met, will improve the situation to some degree. Make sure your demands are specific and achievable – something the other person is likely to agree to rather than reject. And make sure that the demand can be met soon, so that a positive momentum can be generated quickly after the confrontation.

- **Understand the nature of the resistance.** If the other person is being resistant, try to understand its basis: is it really rational, or is it emotional. Do not fight emotional resistance with rational argument. Either coax them into the rational 'zone' with questions or join them in the emotional 'zone' to address the underlying cause of their resistance.

## SKILLS ACTIVITY 12.6: CONFRONTATION

Carry out the confronting interaction that you have selected as the basis for the skills activities in this chapter. They should have provided you with a plan that will help you to face a difficult issue using the technique of feedback and demands.

You must make sure that you practise the skills explored in this chapter in a low-risk situation. If you feel that the case you have been working on in the previous skills activities is inappropriate, identify another situation to use in Skills activity 12.6 which will provide a safer practice opportunity.

We have now reached the end of Part 3. I hope it has achieved its aims of:

- Making you more aware of the instinctive choices you make when you interact with others.
- Giving you greater control over these choices.
- Providing you with alternatives which will increase your effectiveness.

Although all these things will help, changing your behaviour and developing your skills is not easy. It requires patience and practice. To help you plan how you can continue the development that I hope has been happening as you have worked through Part 3, Exercise 12.6 is the same action-planning activity that I suggested you do at the end of Part 2.

## EXERCISE 12.6

Spend a few minutes now reflecting on Part 3 of the book.

- Identify **five** key learning points – things that you have thought about or realized when you were reading Part 3 that you feel will be helpful in improving your performance as a people manager. Write these down in the space provided below.
- Now identify one way that you can apply each of your key learning points at work. These should be specific actions that you are committed to carrying out.

Key learning points                  Actions

1.

2.

3.

4.

5.

# Index